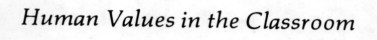

Human Values in the Classroom

HUMAN VALUES

IN THE CLASSROOM:

teaching for personal and social growth

by
Robert C. Hawley, Ed. D.

EDUCATION RESEARCH ASSOCIATES

Amherst, Massachusetts

Published by EDUCATION RESEARCH ASSOCIATES
Box 767, Amherst, Massachusetts 01002

ISBN 0-913636-01-0

Library of Congress Catalog Card Number: 73-77849

Manufactured in the United States of America

CONTENTS

PART ONE:
HUMAN VALUES AND EDUCATION

1. Human Values in the Classroom   1
II. Human Values and Human Needs   6

PART TWO:
A SEQUENCE OF TEACHING CONCERNS

III. Where to Begin   11
IV. Orientation   18
V. Community-Building   21
VI. Achievement Motivation   27
VII. Fostering Open Communication   38
VIII. Information Seeking, Gathering, and Sharing   50
IX. Value Exploration and Clarification   55
X. Planning for Change: Generating Alternatives, Identifying Resources, Decision-Making, Acting on Decisions   70

PART THREE:
NOTES ON TEACHING FOR PERSONAL
AND
SOCIAL GROWTH

XI. Positive Focus   83
XII. Grades and Evaluation   90
XIII. Discipline and Behavior Control   99
XIV. The Classroom as Living Room: Notes on the Use of Space   102
XV. Notes on Creative Thinking   105
XVI. Notes on Role-Taking as a Means of Developing Moral Judgment   109

XVII. Notes on the Authoritarian Personality   112
XVIII. Means Values, End Values, and Social
       Entropy   114

APPENDICES

A. Suggestions for Further Reading   119
B. E R A Teacher Communication Inventory   123
C. An Approach to Inter-Disciplinary Teaching   125
D. Generic Personal Growth Activities   127
E. A Conversation Among Teachers   128
F. Letters from Teachers   134

To Isabel

PART ONE:
HUMAN VALUES AND EDUCATION

I:

HUMAN VALUES IN THE CLASSROOM

"Ladies and gentlemen, I have a special announcement to make. We have a report that a bomb has been planted somewhere in the building. Please do not panic, but proceed to the nearest exit in an orderly manner. Thank you."

One more report of the bomb—the bomb that they never seem to find. We've seen these bomb reports before, in the broken windows of the schoolhouse, the spray-can-painted obscenities on the concrete walls, the vacant eyes of students in class, the reports of truancy, the statistics on drug use, and in the writings of a host of critics of the schools—Silberman, Holt, Herndon, Kozol, Postman and Weingartner, Dennison, and on and on and on. But the ladies and gentlemen have not panicked, and the schools have continued much as before.

This is not to say the schools have not changed—they have. Just as the humans inside the schools—students, teachers, administrators—have changed, so too have the schools changed—in many instances to reflect the growing apathy of the students, the feelings of powerlessness and inadequacy of the teachers, and the exasperation of the administrators.

And yet education continues: on the street corner, in the locker room, on the school bus, in front of the TV, and even in the classroom. Education does go on, but often it is the values that are counter to our human values that are being transmitted: submission to authority, winning by any means, putting up with boredom, the effectiveness of brutality, the importance of trusting nobody.

This book is about teaching human values in the classroom—values such as love, cooperation, trust, acceptance, joy, dignity, respect for individual differences, compromise, truth, understanding, and reverence. These are the human values that moral philosophers and religious leaders have generally agreed upon through the years. These are the human values that must be taught in the classroom and wherever education goes on. They must be taught not merely because of some soft, fuzzy, goody-goody notions that Everyone Should Love One Another, or Cooperation Is Good, and so on. Human values must be taught because they are the key to the survival of the species *homo sapiens*. Teaching human values is teaching survival skills.

This statement seems self-evident to me, but perhaps an additional word or two is needed. If humankind (rather than just some human beings) is to survive for the next century, then the massive competitive value structure which sees only the parts of the global survival puzzle must be dismantled, disarmed, and replaced. This value system which gives rise to the absolute insanity of producing yet another series of nuclear submarines, of annual style changes on ever larger automobiles, of import quota systems, and on, and on, and on, can lead only to the destruction of human society. This value structure, which pits man against man in competition over limited resources, must give way to an understanding that the earth's limited resources must be shared by all if any are to survive. In a society based on human values, man's most precious resource is his fellow man.

It seems equally obvious to me that education in the classroom can play only one part in this shift towards survival values. Television, magazines and newspapers, advertising agencies, political parties, churches, and other educational institutions must play their part. But part of the message of the human values, the survival skills, is the need for trust and interdependence—a willingness to believe in each other, a reliance on others to do their part, and a commitment to do our own part. If the school has a place in the world of tomorrow, if the classroom has a function for the future, it is to teach our young these human values, these survival skills.

Let there be no mistake about what this means for the classroom: There can be no preaching. Skill at tennis is learned by playing tennis; skill at interdependence is learned by working interdependently, and skill at love is learned through loving. It is the teacher's role to foster human values by creating learning opportunities where these values will come into play. And, perhaps even more difficult and more frightening for the teacher, it is the teacher's role to live by the human values that he is teaching.

Fortunately for us, however, these human values *are* skills. They can be taught as skills and learned as skills. No one expects a novice to play tennis like a professional, and we need not expect that we will be perfect at these skills of loving, accepting, trusting, and so forth overnight. Like other skills these take hard work, practice, perseverance; and like other skills these are easier for some to learn than for others. In fact, we can be thankful that acceptance is high on the list of human values, a skill that we can start practicing immediately, accepting ourselves where we are in the acquisition of human values, and accepting others where they are.

But the time is late; the hidden bomb is ticking. Acceptance of the schools as they are does not go to the point of submission. What we wish to change we must first acknowledge the existence of: Then we must find the technical means within our human values to work towards survival.

Plate I:
HUMAN VALUES AS SURVIVAL SKILLS

Love

Cooperation

Trust

Dignity

Respect for individual differences

Acceptance

Unconditional positive regard

Openness

Truth

Honesty

Willingness to help

Understanding

Self-reliance

Joy

Reverence

Health

Adaptability

Integrity

Creativity

(incomplete listing)

II:
HUMAN VALUES AND HUMAN NEEDS

Apathy in the classroom—Teacher after teacher tells the same story: If there were only some way to make students less apathetic, if there were only some way to turn them on. Apathy—the vacant stare, the listless shuffle, the emotionless response—is perhaps the most prevalent symptom of disorder in the school-house today.

Apathy and its brothers, disaffection (the generation gap) and brutality (both physical—vandalism, intimidation, etc., and psychological—the put-down, the sarcasm, the exclusion) are overt symptoms of a system that is very much out-of-order, a system that does not serve us.

Apathy, disaffection, and brutality are the external manifestations of internal feelings of boredom and alienation. Boredom ("The school is meaningless—irrelevant.") and alienation ("Nobody listens.") in turn stem from a sense of powerlessness or lack of control over one's own destiny. Boredom and alienation are the internal symptoms of a craving for the satisfaction of basic needs: needs for safety, belongingness, love, respect, self-esteem; needs for information, knowledge, wisdom.

It is the school's chief function to fill these needs, and in filling them to produce individuals who cannot be bored: individuals who have too high a regard for themselves and too clear a view of the needs of society to find themselves with nothing to do; individuals who have too much assurance of their abilities and their power to allow themselves to sit idle with their minds in neutral. It is the school's function to produce individuals who cannot feel isolated in the midst of mankind—who have the ability to seek out and initiate friendships and associations, the understanding to take part in collaborative efforts, the wisdom to ask for and to give love. It is the school's chief function to produce socially self-actualizing people.

At this point it is appropriate to discuss briefly Abraham Maslow's hierarchy of needs and his theory of social-self-actualization. Maslow theorizes that basic human needs fall into certain categories: the physiological needs for food, warmth, and shelter; the need for safety and security; the need for belongingness; the need for love; the need for respect and self-esteem; and the need for self-actualization. These needs form a natural hierarchy of perceived importance to the individual. That is, when the individual is primarily concerned about filling his physiological needs and his need for safety and security (as we might expect a cave-man to be concerned), then he has little time for or interest in filling the higher needs for belongingness or love; and in fact he may not even be aware of them as needs because his attention is so clearly focused on the more basic needs.

As the lower needs are satisfied, they become less important as motivating forces for the individual, and the individual shifts his focus to the next higher need, which now becomes of great concern to him and which he strives to fulfill. When the person feels safe and secure, and when he perceives his safety as being fairly permanent, then he no longer worries about the need for safety, he no longer plans things that will add to his safety, he no longer strives at establishing a safe situation for himself.

In fact, it could be said that he really forgets his former need for safety as he sees a new need looming in his consciousness: the need for belongingness. Now his motivation will be directed towards gaining belongingness, towards becoming an accepted member of a group.

As the individual gains acceptance and feelings of belongingness, then this need in turn diminishes in importance to him and gradually disappears as a motivating factor, while a new need, the need for love, sweeps into his consciousness and becomes all-important.

And so on up the ladder through the hierarchy of needs until the individual has satisfied all of his basic needs and is able to turn his attention and his energies toward social-self-actualization.[1]

The socially-self-actualizing person is energetic, creative, self-motivating, spontaneous, efficient, accepting, etc. He lives life well and fully, answering to his own inner nature and finding in that nature a call to humanity, to play a useful and helpful part in society. He is acting on human values.

Here then is the task for the schools: To create those conditions where young people can work to satisfy their basic needs so that they may grow towards social-self-actualization. To counteract the effects of alienation by providing for belongingness and love; to counteract the effects of boredom by providing for respect and self-

---

[1]Maslow uses the term *self-actualization,* but he makes it quite clear that genuine self-actualization is also social in nature. Far from merely "doing his own thing," the self-actualizing person sees himself as a socially meliorative agent. To underscore this point I use the term *social-self-actualization.* See Abraham Maslow, *Motivation and Personality,* 2nd ed. (New York: Harper & Row, 1970).

Plate II:
MASLOW'S HIERARCHY OF NEEDS

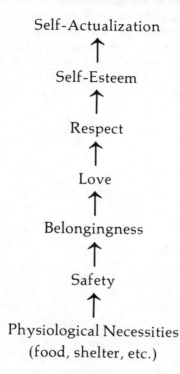

Self-Actualization

↑

Self-Esteem

↑

Respect

↑

Love

↑

Belongingness

↑

Safety

↑

Physiological Necessities
(food, shelter, etc.)

An individual's actions are motivated by a desire to fill his most basic perceived need. Thus a person who feels unsafe is motivated primarily to create a situation of safety for himself. He does not feel the higher need for belongingness until he feels safe on a more or less regular basis. Then, as the old need disappears, a new, higher order need appears, and he acts in ways that will fill his newly felt need for belongingness. And so on up the hierarchy.

esteem: To provide those conditions where personal and social growth can occur at all levels.

NOTE: The Black Panther Party's breakfast program, where children are given breakfast at school, is a striking example of a program designed with an understanding of the basic needs. Hungry children are unable to pay attention to the business of learning because their basic need for nourishment has not been filled. Filling that basic need has provided at least part of the answer.

PART TWO:
A SEQUENCE OF TEACHING CONCERNS

III:
WHERE TO BEGIN

The longest journey begins with a single step.
—Chinese proverb

The problem of reform in education is huge. The social forces against change are so overwhelming and form such a complex network of interrelated pieces that any beginning seems difficult and almost doomed at the start. Take the standard practice of grading, for instance. This is unquestionably one of the most insidious of all current school practices, absolutely destructive of human values. Grading emphasizes competition, extrinsic motivation, external locus of evaluation, rewards for conformity and submission to authority, acceptance and respect conditioned by narrowly defined performance objectives, and an almost inescapable focus on weaknesses. Such emphasis destroys or seriously diminishes the values of cooperation, self-motivation, creativity, self-esteem, unconditional acceptance and respect for human beings, and joy.

Grading is so woven into the warp and woof of the school system that it seems virtually impossible to root out. Parents complain: How will I know how my child is doing? How can I compare my child to others in his class? How will my child get into college without grades? Teachers complain: How can I motivate them without grades? How can I tell what to expect of them? How can we determine who should be on the honor roll? How will they get into college? Students complain: How can I tell how I'm doing? How can I report to my parents? How can I get into college?

Still, we must make a beginning. And we can see already signs of hope—some useful beginnings in such things as the increasing interest in the open classroom, individualized instruction, integrated-day-type classrooms, schools-without-walls, alternative schools, etc. But these beginnings have still left the lives of millions and millions of children unchanged. We must persist, we must step up our efforts, we must persevere: The time is growing short, the time to teach the human values is now, the time to teach survival is at hand.

The rest of this book is an exposition of a sequence of teaching concerns and of related material to help teachers move toward the teaching of human values. Most sequential approaches to education deal with content: a chronological sequence in history, a sequence of themes or genres in literature, a sequence of operations in mathematics, a sequence of conjugations in French, or a sequence from lower to higher orders in biology. The sequence of teaching concerns, on the other hand, deals with the process of learning: It is a sequence of considerations for the teacher to use in planning any lesson, unit, or course:

I.   **Orientation**—Introduction—Why have we all gathered here?

II.   **Community-Building**—How can we get to know each other better so that we can work together better?

III. **Achievement Motivation**—What are our goals? Procedures for reaching those goals? Conditions under which to work toward those goals? What risks are we willing to take in order to attain those goals?

IV. **Fostering Open Communication**—How can we communicate more openly with each other? How can we understand each other better? How can we best share information and ideas in achieving our common goals?

V. **Information Seeking, Gathering, and Sharing**—What do we know and what do we want to know? What information do we have which we can share with each other? Where can we find the information we need?

VI. **Value Exploration and Clarification**—What do we value? What choices can we make which will reflect our values?

VII. **Planning for Change**—How do we want to change? What alternative courses of action are open to us? What resources are available? How can we decide which alternatives and which resources to use? How can we act on our decisions?

While these concerns are overlapping and often reinforcing, they form a definite progression of processes which are useful in organizing any educational undertaking. It is my hope that the sequence will be of practical value to teachers in planning their teaching, as I have found it in mine, and that it will make formal education more comprehensible to students.

The sequence of teaching concerns is a sort of skeleton or guide to help in planning individual lessons, units, terms, or an entire year's work. The concerns are not mutually exclusive: Orientation, for instance, has a lot to do with achievement motivation, and achievement motivation is a value exploration in itself. Developing community involves increasing effectiveness in communication skills, and vice-versa. Nor should the sequence be thought of as rigid and unchangeable: It is designed to help the teacher, not to hamper him. Furthermore, many of the concerns will be continuous ones during the life of the lesson or unit or term. The sequence is only an indication of an appropriate focus for different periods in the life of the class.

For instance, if electricity is the subject of a unit, the teacher might start by asking the class to brainstorm everything they know about electricity, the teacher recording these items on the board. This is a kind of orientation or introduction to the unit. It also serves as a community-building activity, since the brainstorming is a sharing of information with the accent on acceptance and respect for the contributions of all. Then the teacher may ask the students to spend two minutes thinking about and writing down on paper what things they want to know about electricity. Then these questions are put up on the board and the business of goal-setting, or achievement motivation, is begun. Information seeking, gathering, and sharing has also been going on right from the start, and it continues as students attempt to answer each other's questions. Then the teacher may ask the students to look at the board and select the three questions that are most interesting or most important to them, a kind of value exploration and clarification. The students may then form task groups with others who are interested in exploring the same questions. They identify resources for information and proceed to the task of gaining more information on the questions of interest to them. These task groups can later share the results of their study with the class through group reports or displays, etc.

Another unit on electricity might ask the students

to list all the things in their homes that run on electricity, and then to see which they might be willing to eliminate or use less in order to combat environmental pollution. The same sequence of concerns would apply here. The final step would be identifying ways that the members of the class could work for cleaner air.

Like all educational enterprises, the sequence of teaching concerns is most effective when the class is composed of a collection of individuals banding together voluntarily to pursue common ends: The most effective teaching of the above units on electricity would occur in a framework of voluntary education, within which these were elective courses clearly labeled "All About Electricity" or "The Ecological Implications of the Use of Electricity." But since school attendance is (and probably will remain) compulsory in the elementary and most of the secondary years, the next best thing is to offer a wide variety of elective units—of varying lengths, if possible, and including, if possible, self-directed independent study.

Unfortunately this elective system within the compulsory framework is still impossible for most teachers at this time. The general situation is that a teacher and a bunch of students are stuck together for a term or a year and expected to study English, or science, or fifth grade, or whatever. Here the initial concerns of the sequence become much more important: *Orientation—* What are the things that you as students can reasonably expect of me as teacher and of this set of givens (*given* that we're supposed to study English, *given* that I have been given thirty-eight copies of *Silas Marner, given* that I must record a letter grade for each student, etc., etc.)? *Community-building—*How can we get to know each other better so that we can be aware of each other's wants and needs, hopes and fears, and so that we can work better together? *Achievement mo-*

tivation—What goals do we hope to attain during our enforced time together? What are the best procedures for achieving those goals? What are the most suitable rules and conditions to be applied in working towards those goals?

Even within this framework there will be individuals whose goals and perceptions will be so divergent from those of the class as a whole that provision should be made for individual or small-group independent study wherever possible. Perhaps the most difficult problem in setting up this kind of classroom will be with the "traditional student." The traditional student perceives himself as the passive receptor for the knowledge that the teacher dispenses. He feels that it is the teacher's duty to set the goals, procedures, and rules for the class and to enforce compliance through authoritarian measures. Generally he sees community-building as a waste of time, mutual problem-solving as a sign of weakness, and value exploration as an attempt to pry into his private life. Paradoxically, he may also be the most troublesome behavior problem when the teacher tries to lecture or does resort to authoritarian measures.

This attitude is the sign of the beginnings of an authoritarian personality,[1] one who depends upon a hierarchical decision-making structure. This behavior reflects the unconscious attempt of the student to move the locus of responsibility for learning from himself to the teacher, an attempt that the teacher should steadfastly combat. While the teacher has the responsibility of helping the student towards learning and of structuring situations where learning can occur, the locus of responsibility for learning must be squarely on the student.

---

[1]See "Notes on the Authoritarian Personality" in PART THREE below.

While the teacher must accept and recognize the legitimacy of the "traditional student's" concerns, he should structure situations which will lead the student away from this dysfunctional authoritarianism. For instance, the teacher might set up an independent study project that would reflect the traditional goals of the "traditional student": If one of the traditional goals of the student is the study of grammar, the teacher might set up a project where the student can study grammar independently and then be tested on his achievement by some standard test. (This is legitimate not because the study of grammar is necessarily legitimate but because the teacher is helping the student to learn a new way to learn). Then gradually, as the student learns the art of learning, the teacher can help him to take a larger part in setting his own goals and objectives for his learning.

Using the sequence of teaching concerns presented here implies a new and different role for the teacher: He is not merely a dispenser of knowledge. Although he may have expert knowledge in a certain field, and it is proper for him to share this knowledge with his students and even to lecture to them when appropriate, he cannot be expected to possess all the information that his students may want and need. Instead, he is a helper—helping students to diagnose their wants and their needs, helping them to identify information and material resources, helping them to set up useful learning situations, and helping them to develop the skills in creative and critical thinking to take advantage of those learning opportunities. The knowledge that it is vital for this teacher to possess is not so much the knowledge of his subject matter, but the knowledge of how people learn and how he can help them learn.

IV:
ORIENTATION

Any time people get together for purposes of communication, one of the first considerations is orientation—creating a mind set that is conducive to open communication. We tend to do this naturally in informal situations: The small talk that often takes place at the beginning of a business meeting, for instance, has an effect of getting the talkers used to hearing each other's voices and gives them some common ground in knowing one another. The opening few lines of a play or the initial bars of a symphony have the purpose of getting the listener's ear used to the special sounds that are coming from the stage, and at the same time introducing him to the general theme or tone of the piece. The title pictures behind the opening credits of a movie or television show have much the same purpose. Even this paragraph has as one of its purposes orienting the reader to help him understand the content of this section.

In teaching, introducing the lesson or the content of the unit or the work of the term is an important but often neglected consideration. One of the teacher's first tasks is to communicate to the students the goals of the class as the teacher sees them. Any activity that catches the attention of the students and captures their interest in the content of the lesson can be appropriate for orientation.

For instance, to begin a lesson on oxidation, a science teacher can light a candle, watch it burn for a few moments, place it under a bell jar, watch it go out, and then ask: "What made the flame go out?" A social studies teacher can ask which of his students are Roman Catholic, assign them to the back seats in the classroom, and thus begin a unit on religious persecution. Or an English teacher can ask the class to brainstorm all the uses of language as an introduction to a unit on that subject.

Analogies or demonstrations or intriguing problems are all possible ways to introduce a lesson or unit. Variety is important. The chemistry teacher who starts every class with some kind of explosion, for instance, may find that the students soon become accustomed to and blasé about his opening blasts. But more important is the consideration of relevance. The most effective introductions use the students' present knowledge and skills to involve them in the lesson, and the introduction is related to the content in such a way that it and the material presented later interact for cognitive growth. The English teacher above who asks the students to brainstorm the uses of language is getting a picture of the present level of knowledge in the classroom, and he will be able to refer to the brainstormed list throughout the term to make connections between present and future learning. As the social studies class above discusses their emotional reactions to the segregation of Roman Catholic students, they grow cognitively in their awareness of religious persecution.

Planning for orientation involves a diagnosis of the students' needs in regard to the content of the unit and an evaluation of how to make best use of the present level of knowledge existing in the class.

One final consideration in orientation is focusing: Does the introduction focus the subject clearly enough so that it can be dealt with in a significant manner? The science teacher above has focused clearly on the process of oxidation rather than on the uses or the by-products of burning. The English teacher, on the other hand, may need to refine the focus within the broad area of the uses of language. He might do this by asking his students to pick the three uses of language that they consider most interesting or most important, and then move his focus to those. This would have the additional advantage of letting the students help in the focusing process and thus focus on matters of special interest to them. Or the teacher might combine the focus that the students have selected with the concerns that he, from his own experience and knowledge, feels will be valuable to his students at the present time.

V:
COMMUNITY-BUILDING

It's the first day of a new term, and the class is seat-ed in a circle learning each other's names. There is an air of excitement and anticipation as everyone focuses his attention on George. It's George's turn to try to name each of the people who have already had their turn, and to remember the thing that they like to do: "That's swimming Mrs. Smith," he starts, pointing at the teach-er. "That's tennis Jimmy, that's knitting Sally, that's reading Ann, that's eating Sammy, and stick-ball Rosey, roller-skating Roberta, and—and Lois—singing Lois, and I'm, I'm—sleeping George." Everybody laughs, and the focus shifts to the next person in the circle who starts with swimming Mrs. Smith again and tries to name all the people around to himself along with the thing that they like to do. It's not a contest, and there's no penalty for forgetting; in fact, when one of the students gets stuck, the teacher encourages the others to give him help.

This is one of the ways that this teacher is using to get her students to know each other better, to build community.

Far from being a waste of time, building community in the classroom is vital both to the narrow goals of the classroom and to the far goals of education. Com-munity-building is, in fact, a survival skill. One of the clearest messages of the post-World War Two era with its hydrogen bomb, ecology bomb, population bomb, sanity bomb, is that if we fail to develop a world community, we absolutely will not have a world. Perhaps, therefore, the greatest goal of the school is to create in young persons an interest in others in order to secure from them a responsiveness to the real needs of other people and other groups. Only by fostering attitudes of concern and unconditional positive regard for others can we counteract the destructive norms of self-interest that are so prevalent in our society today.

Community in the classroom also helps to achieve the narrow and purely academic goals of the class. There is now a great deal of evidence that when a high level of attraction exists among the students and between students and teacher, and when patterns of influence and friendship are dispersed widely among the members of the class, then the attitudes of the students toward the academic goals of the class are more positive, students take more satisfaction from pursuing the goals of the class, and academic achievement is likely to be increased.

Building community helps to fill basic human needs at many levels—security, belongingness, love, respect, self-esteem. When there is little feeling of community in a classroom, students are likely to feel anxiety, hostility, self-doubt, rejection. And all these negative feelings are likely to contribute to unconstructive, nonproductive behavior—behavior which, paradoxically, is likely to be self-perpetuating, as teacher disapproval may lead to more feelings of self-doubt and rejection which in turn triggers acting out or other unconstructive behavior, which again causes teacher reaction in an ever-expanding negative spiral.

On the other hand, community decreases anxiety and increases feelings of security and belongingness. Then as each member is seen in the light of the unique set of characteristics which he brings to the group, mutual respect and feelings of self-esteem develop. Thus, since a young person develops most of his self-concepts through the mirror of his relationships with others, the quality of trust, respect, and affection that he feels from others has a direct impact on the degree to which he uses his intelligence and other vital energies in pursuing his goals.

Furthermore, peer influence and support is important in helping the young person move from adult-dependency towards self-sufficiency. Classroom community can be a significant stepping-stone in this process of cutting the apron strings. Where the importance of community and positive peer-relations is understood, there is more chance for an easy transition, less likelihood that the movement towards independence will be cataclysmic and destructive.

Building community in the classroom takes time and commitment. It is an ongoing process that must continue throughout the life of the class. Here are some of the characteristics that a teacher can work for in creating community:

1. Students share influence with each other and with the teacher.

2. There is a high level of attraction for the class as a whole and among individual members of the class: Members like the class and each other.

3. The attitudes of the members and the norms of the group support the goals of the class.

4. The attitudes of the members and the norms of the group support and encourage individual differences among the members of the class.

5. There is open and honest communication both among the students and between the students and the teacher.

6. There is a feeling of shared responsibility among

the students and with the teacher both to maintain and improve the community and also to further the goals of the class.[1]

In building community the teacher must be quite explicit about the importance of community to both the near and the far goals of education, and his commitment to building community must shine through and permeate the class. The more the teacher can elicit ways of building community from the class, and the more he can involve the members of the class in the responsibility for developing and maintaining community, the more likely it is that a high degree of community can be attained. It may be useful for the teacher to conduct periodic or continuing discussions on "Where are we as a group?" Other teachers may take a more intuitive approach, structuring activities and tasks that will lead the class toward better community.

Specific problems may require special measures by the teacher. For instance, where there is specific rejection of one or several students by others, role-playing may be useful to help develop empathy and understanding. The teacher might place an open chair at the front of the room, give the chair a fictitious name, and then ask the members of the class to think of the things that that person could do that would "turn people off." As the students contribute, the teacher notes each item briefly on the board. Then a second chair is placed at the front and the process is repeated with "things that would make others like you." Now these two chairs engage in an imaginary meeting. The teacher sets up the situation: "Suppose these two people met in the hall. Who would start the conversation, and what would he

---

[1]For a more complete treatment of this and other related subjects see Richard A. Schmuck and Patricia A. Schmuck, *Group Processes in the Classroom* (Dubuque, Iowa: Wm. C. Brown Co., 1971).

say?'' When someone contributes the opening line, then the teacher says, "And how would the other respond?'' The open-chair role-play is continued for two or three minutes, and then the class discusses what went on and ways that the two could have a better understanding of each other.

Using the open chairs instead of actual students gives a certain amount of protection to individuals who may wish to pose problems or state points-of-view but who do not have sufficient ego-strength to role-play in front of a class. After the initial "open chair" session, some students may be willing and eager to sit in the chairs and play the roles. This is often a productive extension of the activity.

Another common problem in classroom community occurs at the beginning of a term or year where there are several new students in the group. For this situation the teacher might ask the class to think of instances when they have come into a group for the first time. Then the teacher asks for volunteers who will recount their experiences and tell how it felt to be new in a group. Then the teacher asks the students to reflect individually and write down three or four questions that they might ask in order to get to know somebody. After all have had time to think of a few questions, the teacher asks all the students to stand and then go to a person that they don't know well or at all and spend four minutes getting to know that person better, using some of the questions that they have constructed. At the end of the four minutes, the teacher asks the pairs to spend two more minutes working together trying to identify things that they have in common. Several possibilities are open at this point. The teacher could ask the students to leave their partners, find new partners and repeat the process; or he could ask them to join their pairs into groups of four where each person introduces his partner to the other members of the group; or he could conduct a general discussion, focusing on things that the students may have in common, the feelings that people have in a new situation, and ways that the class can become a better community.

VI:
ACHIEVEMENT MOTIVATION

Overheard in the faculty room: "He's just not motivated." "If only I could find a way to motivate them!" "How can we get them motivated?"

Achievement motivation—seemingly a mystical talent, or an elusive trick, or a long sought-after button to push to get students started—has been the subject of anguish and concern in schools for generations. What motivates people to do things—or not do them—is still often a mystery, but in the last dozen years or so, research has begun to throw some light on the subject, and we can make some tentative conclusions as to what does motivate at least some people, and what this means for teaching and teachers.

First, however, it is important to point out the difference between *motivating* a student and *controlling* him. When a teacher says, "How can I motivate Johnny to do his math?" the teacher may, in fact, be looking for a means of controlling Johnny's behavior so that Johnny does what teacher says to do. That is not motivation. Motivation comes from the inside—all motivation is self-motivation. If it is motivation to do math homework that is needed, then it is Johnny's own will and desire to do that homework that the teacher must stimulate in order to motivate him. Somehow Johnny must perceive the task as worth doing, either because of the intrinsic excitement of making discoveries about the physical world around him, or because of an extrinsic factor such as the perceived usefulness of the skill acquired, the desirability of pleasing the teacher, the importance of getting a good grade, the fear of parental disapproval, or some other related consequence of doing the homework.

This consideration imposes certain limitations on what sorts of activities are susceptible to motivation techniques by the teacher. Certainly, the more intrinsically exciting or interesting or the more immediately relevant the task is perceived to be, the more likely the possibility of motivating the student. At the other extreme, the more arcane or inane the task is perceived to be by the student, the more extreme will be the motivating measures required by the teacher—inducements such as lollipops, transistor radios, days off from school (Can you believe it?), or conversely, character defamation, whipping, threats of capital punishment.

Another preliminary consideration is the complexity of motivation in any instance. There is no single motivating force within the individual. Motivation is made up of a complex bundle of drives, attitudes, habits, and innate characteristics. Just as individuals are different in color of hair or shape of nose, just as one person may thrive on sardines while another is made physically ill by the mere thought of them, so individuals have different physiological and psychological personalities in regard to motivation. (There is immense variation, for instance, in the amount of adrenalin which different individuals are capable of producing, and a person who has always had plenty of food, clothing, shelter, love, security, and respect will have a different psychology from the homeless orphan's).

With these preliminary considerations of control and individual differences in mind, let us take a look at some of the factors which can contribute to achievement motivation in the classroom. And then we will delineate some techniques which may be useful to classroom teachers.

There are three general factors in establishing the motivational climate in the classroom: The *goals* for the class, the *procedures* which are to be used in reaching those goals, and the general *conditions and rules* for work within the classroom. High motivation in the classroom is likely to occur when the goals, procedures, and conditions or rules of the class are clearly understood by all, and where there is an honest sense of class participation in setting the goals, determining the procedures, and delineating the conditions and rules.

The key is in the correspondence between teacher-perception and student-perception in goals, procedures, and conditions. I recall that when I was teaching English in junior high school, my goals as an English teacher were perfectly clear to me: They were to help students learn to use their language with facility and enjoyment—but it never occurred to me to tell that to the students. Nor did it occur to me to ask whether the procedures which I set up were leading towards those goals, and it certainly never occurred to me to ask the students what their own goals for the class were!

There are at least two possibilities which might have occurred had I merely shared my goals with my students or asked them what their goals were. First, I might have clarified for them just why we were doing what we were doing, and they might have given me some indication as to the degree to which I was reaching my goals in their eyes; and second, my students might have pointed out some other or more clearly defined goals that were important (and thus motivating) factors to them—such short term goals as getting a high score on the College Board exam, getting on the honor roll, or not being too bored in class; or such long term goals as learning to write business letters, understanding who they are, or figuring out how to beat the stock market. These student goals would have been clearly compatible with my goals, and they would have been useful in giving direction to my lesson planning and to my self-evaluation. And at the same time, because we as a class would have been working on goals that were more clearly defined or more closely linked with the personal goals of the students, many of the students would have been better motivated towards the work of the class.

This does not mean that every class must be planned on the spot around the extemporaneous goals laid out by the students. I'm not suggesting that Algebra Two might become a course in sports cars, or Latin One a seminar on the Beatles. Such a situation would quickly lead to chaos, as no advanced planning or ordering of materials would be possible, and there would be a strong tendency for fadism or intellectual mediocrity. The teacher of Algebra Two, for instance, can clearly delineate his objectives, both immediate and philosophical, to the class. Within the framework of those goals and whatever modifications of them the teacher is willing or able to make, however, an attention to the goals of the students—be they to pass the course, to get a seven hundred on the College Board Exam, to not be too bored, to learn quantum theory—is likely to result in an improved motivational atmosphere in the class.

There are many ways to elicit the goals of students as an aid in planning a course. Simplest is to ask them, "What are your goals, your hopes for being here?" This simple directness may leave students bewildered and non-plussed because they have been trained to be passive receptors rather than active participants in the class. Often students have had so little opportunity to take part in the planning of their education that they may consider the teacher who asks such a question just a little odd. And too, students may feel that their hopes and goals will not have any impact on the conduct of the class in any case. "No hopes, no disappointments," wrote one of my students when asked to write her hopes for the class at the first meeting of the year.

Another procedure is to ask the class to meet in groups of four or five for ten minutes to discuss their hopes for the term. At the end of the ten minutes the groups are asked to isolate four or five hopes that seem important to them, and then one person in each group makes a brief oral report of those hopes. The group report makes it easier to elicit those hidden hopes: "Someone in our group said that he hoped that he wouldn't be too bored." "We hoped that we would make a good grade." "Someone in our group hoped that we would be dismissed two minutes early so that we would be first in the lunch line." These are often among the real hopes of students; and to the degree that they are openly stated and explicit, there is less likelihood of subversion or an undercurrent of hostility in the class. The teacher may not be able to fulfill some of the hopes, but his awareness of them may change the climate of the class: "Well, I can't let you go two minutes before the end of the period, but I promise that I will never hold you after the bell."

Such an awareness of the formerly hidden hopes of students releases the energy that is normally channeled into anxiety ("Will he let us out on time?") so that it can be channeled into the formal goals of the class (learning the causes of the Civil War, or whatever).

A third goal-setting procedure is to collect the goals of the class either from individuals or from group reports and then to duplicate them and pass them out to the members of the class along with a duplicated copy of the teacher's own goals. These two sheets can serve as continuing points of reference as the class works out the procedures for reaching those goals.

The one danger in goal-setting is that the goals may be seen as final and unchanging. As with procedures and rules, goals should be seen as tentative—to be changed when appropriate in the light of new information or circumstances. Perhaps one of the most important functions of the class should be the continuing re-evaluation of its own goals as the term progresses.

One additional consideration in setting goals: The goals must be seen as realistic and attainable. Only a madman would undertake to climb Mount Everest without the kind of pre-planning that would give him a reasonable chance at success. The wise horse refuses the jump that it sees as too high. Students have little motivation to attempt things that they know they are going to fail at. Achievement motivation generally increases as the challenge increases, but when the goal is seen no longer as challenging but rather as threatening failure, then motivation drops off. Just as in mountain-climbing, where careful planning and setting of procedures reduces the chance of failure and makes the climb seem possible, so in learning, the planning of procedures will often make the goals seem more realistic and attainable.

In determining the procedures to be used in working towards the goals of the class, two factors are important: First, different students learn in different ways, so that the wider the variety of learning modes employed, the more likely it is that each student will find one that fits his style and thus be motivated towards the goals of the class. Second, students generally have an extremely limited view of possible learning styles—often thinking that lecturing, reading, memorizing, and directed discussion are the only valid learning procedures. Here the teacher will need to introduce the class to a wider variety of learning styles and also show the students that learning can take place in contexts other than the conventional ones.

Students have often been trained, for instance, that important learning can take place only when the teacher is present, directing and programming the instruction. Also students often think of learning in the narrow context of acquiring and storing bits of information for easy retrieval at the teacher's demand. In helping students to expand their concepts of what learning is, the teacher might ask students to discuss how they learned to walk, talk, ride a bicycle, throw a ball, find their way home, buy things with money, run the television set or record player, etc. The class might try to identify as many people as possible who could be called "teacher"— storekeepers, brothers and sisters, parents, priests, authors, actors, and so on.

Then the teacher might list alternative learning styles—class discussion, lecture, reading and report, large and small group discussion with and without leaders, group independent study, individual independent study, film, group or individual field work, case study, simulation, role-play, skits. And the class can discuss its experiences with each and the possible uses of each style for the goals established by the class. Finally, the teacher can set up situations where students can experience those learning styles that they are not familiar with so that they will then be able to choose among a wider range of alternatives.

Two special considerations in setting procedures are identifying the risks involved in pursuing the goal and structuring tasks so that the risks involved are acceptable to the students concerned. Simply put, the assignment of ten problems in arthmetic demands a risk on the part of the student. It is a risk of his time, energy, good will, and often his self-esteem. Here the teacher can help to motivate his students in four ways.

The first way is by setting clear limits to the size of the risk that is to be undertaken. Thus where an assignment of ten problems may seem to be a risk of an unknown quantity of time and effort to a particular student, the teacher might ask the students to commit to the task of learning math a limited period of time, such as half-an-hour, per night and ask them to practice carefully by doing problems on page such-and-such for that half-hour (just as figure skaters and concert pianists often practice a given amount of time per day). The risk of time and energy is thus clearly limited, and the fear of failure to achieve perfection is eliminated, perhaps to be replaced by the challenge of seeing how many problems one can do accurately in the allotted time.

Second, the teacher can suspend or reduce the threatening consequences of taking a risk. For example, while reading one's weekly composition in front of the whole class may involve the possibility of too great a loss of self-esteem for some students to risk, if the teacher sets up small work groups where each member reads his composition to the rest of the group, then the risk to self-esteem may be reduced to the point where the student will be willing to try.

Third, he can give permissions for students to take unusual risks, risks that the students might hesitate to take without permission. Most students would be reluctant to stand in front of a supermarket and interview the shoppers, for instance; but with a tape recorder in hand and the teacher's "permission," this can be an important learning experience.

Finally, the teacher can work to show the connection between the risk involved and the reward that can be attained by taking that risk. Whether it be the joy of a job well done, the usefulness of a new and relevant skill, a high grade on a report card, or a transistor radio, whenever the reward is perceived to be important enough to justify the risks, the student will be motivated toward the task.

In regard to the conditions and rules under which the class will work toward its goals, three factors affect the motivational climate of the classroom. First, where the rules are clear and understandable to all, members of the class are unlikely to be anxious about inadvertently getting into trouble by unintentionally breaking a rule. Second, where the rules and conditions can be seen by the students to be based on the objective requirements of the situation rather than upon the seeming whims of the teacher, then the class will be more likely to understand the reasons for the limitations imposed upon them. Where rules and conditions of the class are clearly determined by a concern for the health, safety, welfare, and morals of the members of the class rather than by the arbitrary likes and dislikes of the teacher, then the psychic energy that is often spent in fighting rules and objecting to conditions can go into motivation toward the goals of the class. And third, to the degree that students share in establishing rules and determining the conditions under which they will work, they will be additionally motivated toward the goals of the class.

Periodic class meetings can be helpful in establishing and re-evaluating the rules and conditions of the class. The class should sit in a circle with the teacher included and with no other agenda than the rules and conditions. The teacher should direct the course of the meeting as little as possible, responding honestly to questions put to him and commenting on the feasibility of changes in conditions which are suggested. The teacher should be careful to refrain from making commitments that he may be unable to keep, and he should be as open as possible about the restraints under which he himself works. For instance, he may be unable to allow the students to go individually to poll the customers in a nearby shopping center because of parental concern over safety. Or he may not be able to arrange to lengthen the class periods, reduce the heat in the room, move to a room with a carpeted floor, etc. And yet he should be open to suggestions as to how these may be done.

One special condition that the teacher can have some control over is the setting up of a climate where the win-lose, highly competitive atmosphere is reduced or eliminated. Except in the specialized case where the competition is perceived as a game, such as in a spelling bee, the aura of competition does little to stimulate even the perennial winners and adds another layer of threat to those who often lose. Where the grading system requires that students be compared so that some receive A's and some F's on a particular task, then the student's motivation decreases as his expectation of being cast among the losers increases. On the other hand, where tasks are seen as cooperative ventures where each individual can contribute his part and can share in the rewards of the group accomplishment, then motivation, especially the motivation of the less able, tends to increase.

Certainly all of these motivation techniques take time. A question that the teacher must face early in the course is how much time should be diverted from the content of the course into processes such as achievement motivation, opening up communication, and the like. It is the strong opinion of the author that most teachers devote too little rather than too much time to these useful processes. Clearly, well-motivated students learn more and learn faster than poorly-motivated ones, and the time taken to improve the motivational climate of the class can be said to be time invested for future earnings rather than time wasted with no profit.

Motivation is a diffuse bundle of emotional forces that compel an individual toward action. Ultimately it is based upon the individual's self-concepts and his values, for a person will be emotionally drawn to pursue those goals which he values. The stronger the individual's self-concepts, the more positive he is of his strength and abilities, the more likely he is to be motivated to act on his values. Here is the importance of a meaningful and relevant curriculum, for it is by engaging in meaningful action and pursuing meaningful goals that the individual grows in self-concept. Where the individual can see himself engaging in socially significant work, and where the individual can see himself as responsible to himself and to others as a result of that work, he learns to value himself and his ability—he becomes self-motivated.

VII:
FOSTERING OPEN COMMUNICATION

"We must learn how to improve our communications!" "If only we had been able to communicate better!" "Communications, communications, that's the important thing!" These are the clichés that fly around the room at faculty meeting time. And like all clichés, they touch on a real and important concern. And yet somehow, communication doesn't improve much. The old misunderstandings still persist. More and more English curriculums have become "Communications" curriculums, with Communications I replacing the old English I. The content, however, is often much the same—composition focusing heavily on mechanical correctness, literature focusing on an exploration of the deeper meanings of the great works of great authors. And yet teachers and administrators are neither villainous nor stupid. Overwhelmingly they are intelligent and hard-working people who desire to become more effective, but people who lack the information to improve their skills in communication.

Communication is a skill which is at once simple and complex. Simply put, communication is nothing more than sending and receiving messages. But the complexity lies in the transmission—the sending and receiving. For every message carries with it a certain amount of "noise"—that is, extra information not under the conscious control of the sender and often not under the conscious control of the receiver. This information serves to change the conscious intent of the message sender so that the message received is altered—diminished, enlarged, modified—in some way not the same as the message sent. Improving communication skills, then, requires an awareness of the variety and scope of this "noise" and skills for reducing or controlling the "noise" in the message.

Jack Gibb, a social psychologist and originator of the TORI method of interpersonal development, has identified several types of noise which produce defensive reactions in receivers and diminish the effectiveness of a communication. He sees communication as a "people process" rather than a "language process"— that is, a fundamental interaction among people. In order to increase the effectiveness of communication, one must make changes in interpersonal relationships. In the cases that Gibb concerns himself with, this means changing the relationship between the sender and the receiver so that the receiver does not feel threatened by the communication. Threat closes the windows of perception and turns the eye inward upon the self and away from the message and sender. When a person feels threatened by a communication, he starts to think how best he can defend himself, what his appearance may be to others, how he can show himself and his actions in a more favorable light, how he can avoid an expected attack.

For instance, when a teacher asks, "Where have you been?" the student might feel that this is a genuine request for information based on the teacher's interest in the lives of other people, or, more likely, the student may perceive a threat, that is an implied condemnation of his past behavior. If the student does feel threatened, he will start all sorts of defense mechanisms—withdrawal, submission, counter-attack—all of which diminish the degree to which he and the teacher can exchange messages rationally and effectively. Furthermore, the student's defensive behavior is likely to raise a defensive posture in the teacher, who then appears more menacing to the student, whose response may again heighten the defensiveness in the teacher in a continuing spiral.

Gibb has identified six categories of behavior which tend to raise defensiveness in communication, and six contrasting behaviors which lead to open, supportive communication. I have modified Gibb's categories to produce a series of six continuums along which a communication can be rated, from highly defense-producing to highly open and supportive. These continuums are as follows:

Defense-producing	**Supportive**
Evaluative	Descriptive
Controlling	Cooperative
Hidden	Open
Neutral	Empathetic
Superior	Equal
Certain	Provisional

Evaluative—Descriptive: Messages, both verbal and nonverbal which appear to evaluate the listener are defense-raising. The put-down is a good example of a highly evaluative kind of communication which is popular among students: "Wouldn't you know it?" or "That's just like you!" or "Nice going." Or non-verbally hitting the forehead with the butt of the palm and rolling the eyes. But there are other forms of evaluative communication that are more subtle. In fact, the use of evaluative communication in our culture is so common that expressions which the receiver will regard as non-judgmental are difficult to frame. Statements of value judgment often are inferred to be evaluative, that is appreciating the receiver for agreement, depreciating him for non-agreement: For instance, "I think all this recycling business is nonsense." Or "Anyone who voted for Gene McCarthy is a hopeless idealist." In either case a person not agreeing with the speaker may feel threatened and therefore defensive. Many questions, too, have an implied evaluation in the degree to which the answer conforms with the questioner's expectations.

Descriptive communication, on the other hand, is less likely to arouse defensiveness and more likely to engender a climate of mutual supportiveness. Messages which present feelings, ideas, or facts, but which do not imply that the receiver should change his attitudes or behavior can be seen as at the descriptive end of the continuum. "I" statements generally fall at the descriptive end of this continuum. "I feel upset with your behavior," or "I feel that I need more information before I can decide about that" describe the sender's condition while "You're making me upset," or "You haven't told me what I need to know," evaluate the other's actions.

Controlling—Cooperative: Messages which are perceived as attempts to control the receiver, to influence attitudes, change behaviors, or restrict activities are defense-raising. And the more subtle the controlling message is perceived to be, the greater the degree of defensiveness. While an overt attempt at control elicits either acceptance and compliance or open rejection, a message which is perceived to be a subtle attempt at control elicits either covert resentment or boot-legged non-compliance, or both. "Don't you all want to do well in your next school?" or "I'm sure everybody really wants to do well on the test," or "Didn't we agree at the beginning of the year that we wouldn't chew gum in class?" are all transparent attempts to control values or behavior.

When the message indicates a desire on the part of the sender to engage in a cooperative enterprise, then the message generally creates the same spirit of cooperation in the receiver. The message implies a willingness on the part of the sender to allow the receiver to set his own goals, make his own decisions, and evaluate his own progress, or else to collaborate with the sender in the process: "What's the best way to handle this?" or "How do you want to divide up the research for this report?" or "Let's see how we can work this out," or "What can I do to help you finish this composition?"

In schools this aspect of communication is highly related to achievement motivation, for students who are allowed to share in the goal-setting, decision-making, and evaluation processes in the class are likely to be the most successfully motivated. Implicit in this consideration, however, is the caution that the teacher who feigns cooperative goal-setting, decision-making, or evaluation in order to control students towards his own ends will be seen as subtly attempting control, and thus will produce defensiveness in his students.

Hidden—Open: When the receiver feels that the message is ambiguous or has a hidden purpose, then his defenses are raised. This is especially true when the receiver feels that the sender is using a strategy to involve the receiver or to make him think that he is making his own decisions. Psychologists who set up a test which ostensibly tests for one thing while secretly testing for something else often find a resentment when the subject discovers that he's been tricked. And teachers who ask students to bring in rock music to listen to and then force the class to write a composition about it can be resented for the same reason.

At the other end of the continuum, a message which is seen as open and uncomplicated is likely to reduce the defensiveness of a receiver. When the purposes of the message sender are clear, and when his responses seem spontaneous and unrehearsed, then the receiver becomes more open to the message. In a classroom context this would indicate that the teacher who is clear about his goals and about why he is asking students to follow certain procedures is the most likely to elicit student cooperation. Such openness implies, too, that he will be spontaneous and open in response to the various demands made on him by the class. Thus he needs to be flexible and willing to modify the goals and procedures of the class in the light of student expectations. Open communication by its very nature requires a certain provisionalism and problem-solving orientation, a flexibility to react to the open communication of others.

Neutral—Empathetic: When the tone or content of the message implies a lack of concern for the welfare of the receiver, then the receiver becomes defensive, as he begins to search himself to find out why he is not valued or perceived as worthy by the message sender. The classroom teacher who hides all emotion generates a feeling of lack of involvement among students, and in a self-fulfilling cycle, students will be less caring toward the welfare of the teacher, which in turn will raise the teacher's defensiveness and feelings of unworthiness.

In contrast, where the message sender conveys a feeling of empathy and caring towards the receiver, the receiver feels supported, and his defenses are reduced. Teachers who show their concern for the personalities and welfare of their students engender feelings of trust and responsiveness in their students.

Superior—Equal: When a message receiver feels that the sender is communicating to him from a position of superiority in intellectual ability, power, wealth, social position, or physical strength, then his defenses are raised. In a class where the teacher makes a difficult problem look easy for himself to do, the students react by feeling less worthy or by tuning out or by feeling jealous of the teacher's accomplishments. And when the teacher uses his position of power to force the students to do something "because I say so," then the students perceive the teacher as not willing or able to receive feedback or to make changes in behaviors or attitudes.

Real differences in power or status may exist, but the effective message sender is the one who creates a climate where these differences do not seem to be an important part of the relationship. When the person with high power or status is perceived to be willing to engage in mutual problem-solving and in a give-and-take of ideas, then the receiver is more open to his messages. This does not mean that all teachers must go on a first-name basis, but it does imply that teachers who put aside their trappings of authority and power are more effective communicators in the classroom. This kind of knowledge is implicit in the behavior of many teachers of young children, who go to great efforts to bring themselves down to their students' heights by sitting in low chairs or on the floor.

Certain—Provisional: The message sender who seems absolutely certain of his correctness, who knows all the answers, who needs no help or additional information is a well-known defense producer. The teacher who is never wrong or must always have an answer for everything blocks himself off from his students, makes it apparent to his students that they can have no effect on him. Thus he raises their defenses and feelings of powerlessness.

On the other hand, the message sender who shows that he is interested in experimenting, in finding answers, in problem-solving and exploring, in gaining new information, communicates a willingness to share with others. And this in turn engenders a feeling of openness and support from others.

Taken together the six categories at one end of the

continuum represent one personality type—descriptive, cooperative, open, empathetic, equal, provisional— while the six categories at the other end represent quite another—evaluative, controlling, hidden, neutral, superior, certain. But teachers who want to become more effective communicators can pick one or two areas where they see themselves near the defense-raising end of the continuum and then try different behaviors which might move them toward the other end of that continuum.

A teacher who rates himself near the *superior* end of the *superior-equal* continuum, for instance, might try to think what specific behaviors in the classroom lead students to perceive him as superior: tone of voice, style of dress, use of authority symbols such as the teacher's desk or podium. Then the teacher can pick one behavior to modify—moving away from the teacher's desk, for example. As the teacher tries out new behaviors, he can find out which ones are useful in meeting his objective of communicating more effectively.

As the teacher adopts new behaviors, his relationship with his students changes. He begins to see them in new ways, and he begins to respond to them in different ways, so that his attitudes toward his students, himself, and teaching change. Changed behavior often precedes change in attitudes and beliefs. As the teacher relates to his students in new and more supportive ways, his personality changes: He becomes more open and supportive.

Looking at communication from another angle, I have found three pointers tremendously useful in understanding this complex process. The first is that *almost every question has a statement underlying it.* It is generally useful to identify the underlying statement as an aid in answering the question. Take a simple question such as "What did you think of that movie?" This could really be saying, "I want you to commit yourself first so that I can agree with you," or "I'm really puzzled by the movie," or "I really liked the movie but don't want to risk admitting it unless you liked it too," or "I want to know if you are as good a critic as I am," or "I'm embarrassed by silence, let's talk," or many more things. By phrasing the statement as a question, the questioner has forced the listener to try to determine which of the possible underlying statements he should respond to.

Here is another example: "Why did Hamlet spare Claudius while he was praying?" Does the teacher want to know whether the students were paying attention in class on the day that he talked about that? Or does he want to know if the students have read the passage in the anthology of criticism which discusses the point? Or does the teacher want to know if the students have any original ideas on the topic? Or does he want to know if the students can organize and express themselves in written form with a minimum of errors in spelling and punctuation and with a vigorous style?

One way to improve communication is to become more aware of what our concerns really are when we ask a question and to try to identify those concerns to our listeners as fully as possible. Another way to improve communication is to listen for questions which might reflect underlying concerns of others, and then to ask for clarification of the concerns which underlie the questions.

A second useful pointer is to *identify introjectors*—those questions and statements which try to force a value position on another person: "We all can agree that civil defense is important, can't we?" or "But don't you believe that the home is the most important influence in the early years?" or "I think that we are all agreed that everyone should do some work for his own self-esteem." These are verbal strong-arm tactics which may gain overt acceptance or agreement but which often lead to underlying resentment. Changing these to "I" statements is more likely to lead to an open exchange of ideas, less likely to raise defensiveness: "I feel that civil defense is important," "I think that the home is the most important influence in the early years," "I think that everyone should do some work for his own self-esteem."

The third pointer is to *be aware of put-downs or killer statements:* "You don't really mean that, do you?" or "Come on, be serious, you can't really feel that way," or "How many times do I have to tell you?" or "Can't you get it right just this once?" or "Not that way, stupid!" These statements are defense-raising because they attack the person rather than the problem.

The most common response of a person who has been assaulted by a put-down is to look for deficiencies in the personality of the one who put him down. The receiver and sender become locked in an ego conflict, attacking each other's personalities rather than engaging in a cooperative venture in solving a problem. The eventual outcome of such an encounter is likely to be one of three possibilities: continued hostility, retreat and withdrawal on the part of one of the persons, or submission of one to the other. Even though one may eventually gain his will over the other, the possibilities for cooperative problem-solving will have been lost.

Being aware of killer statements and put-downs is the first step of improving communication in this area. When an individual becomes aware of his own unintentional use of put-downs so that he can avoid using them, he will begin to become a more effective communicator. When he can identify put-downs and killer statements in others, then he can work towards channeling the relationship back away from ego attack towards solving the problem. Rather than take the bait and escalate the ego conflict, he can indicate his willingness to share in cooperative problem-solving. "Let's try to work this out," "Let's try to deal with this problem," "I feel that we have a problem here that we can work on," "I'm beginning to feel defensive—let's see if we can focus on the problem," are all possible ways to re-channel the energies away from conflict back towards collaboration.

Being aware of put-downs and killer statements is perhaps the most important step in changing the climate of the classroom towards one of openness and support. Students are masters of the put-down. They learn it from their peers, from their adult acquaintances, from television; and they use it unsparingly on each other without recognizing the unwitting damage that they may be doing to others and themselves. And students have developed the non-verbal put-down to a high level. Smacking the forehead with the hand while rolling the eyes back is a favorite form of non-verbal put-down. Others range from dramatically throwing up the hands to raising an eyebrow ever so slightly.

The classroom teacher can foster an awareness of put-downs in many ways: by discussion and explanation, by brainstorming all the possible verbal put-downs that students can think of and then all the non-verbal ones, by role-playing situations where one person is trying to put down another, or by asking students to keep a record of all the put-downs that they hear in the course of a morning. Then through discussion and role-play the class can work on identifying and trying out ways of dealing with the put-downs so as not to get back at the other but to channel energy towards finding useful solutions to problems.

This is a question of the individual's becoming more aware of his own energies and how they are used and then making a conscious decision to take control of his own energies to use them so that they serve him as he wants them to. For instance, when a person has just been put down by another, there will usually be an unconscious desire to get back at the other, and at least some of the victim's energy is drained off in planning schemes for revenge and in anxiety over whether or not he will be able to use his schemes. If the energy thus drained off causes the individual to be less able to accomplish other more important objectives, then his response to the put-down will have served to reduce his own power and his control over himself and his environment. If he is able to understand this, he may be better able to rechannel that energy toward his own important objectives.

If his most important objective is, in fact, to get back at the one who put him down, then he should be aware of this fact, too. And he should question himself as to whether or not this revenge is the best way to use his energy in the long run. My opinion, as I suspect you have guessed, is that it is not—that the energy thus spent could be better used in growth-fostering activities such as enlisting the cooperation and support of the attacker and thus leading to growth for both. In any event, the more aware the individual is of his motivations, the more likely it is that he can use his power to his own advantage, the more control he will have over his own existence.

In the last analysis, all the dimensions of communication discussed in this chapter deal with the use of energy, for when a person uses part of his energy in defending himself against another, then he has less energy available to support the other in a collaborative venture. The "noise" which I talked about at the beginning of the chapter is anything which channels energy away from the business of understanding and supporting each other. For communication really means finding understanding and support.

VIII:
INFORMATION
SEEKING, GATHERING, AND SHARING

How many magazines do you subscribe to? And how many do you read? How long is your list of "must read" books? If you are like most of the people that I know, you subscribe to more magazines than you can read, and you have a "must read" list that grows longer rather than shorter. Four hundred years ago there were about one thousand books published in a single year; now there are one thousand books published each day. One of my basic anxieties is that I will miss some vital piece of information—a new research finding, a breakthrough in medicine, a new tax ruling. I suspect that it is this basic anxiety which accounts for the gigantic success of the *Reader's Digest* enterprises.

We are virtually glutted with information, and yet our methods of processing information remain primitive and inefficient. Furthermore, our schools seem to be locked into a conspiracy to limit the variety and quantity of information available to students and to perpetuate inefficient methods of information processing. The use of textbooks, for example, insures that all students will get the same limited amount of information on a given subject, and that they will have little opportunity to question the certainty of that information in comparison with other sources. The practice of having the entire class read the same poem, the same novel, the same short story limits the variety and amount of cultural and aesthetic information available in the classroom and reinforces the conception of cultural unity and reverence for certain "classics." Furthermore, these practices of limiting information sources have the effect of making students less valuable to each other as resources. Since they have all studied the same texts, they have nothing new to tell each other, and so must rely on the teacher as the provider of all important information and knowledge.

Looking back over my own junior high school teaching experience, I recall that some of the best classes, classes when the students seemed most alert, responsive, and excited, were book report times when each student brought in the book that he had been reading, held it up for all to see, and gave a minute or minute-and-a-half review and critique. These book report classes always ended with students borrowing each other's books or swapping or going out to find another copy of the most popular books.

This is not to deny the value of some common assignments. Classes often work more effectively together when there is some common body of knowledge among the group, where there are certain concepts and assumptions held in common as starting points. As I have mentioned, the root word of *communication* is *common*. We communicate better with those with whom we have something in common. What is needed is flexibility.

In a world where information sources are so varied and abundant, where we are threatened with being swamped and confused and misled by information overload, one of the most important skills which we can teach our children is collaborative information processing. What is overwhelming to one may be comprehensible to a group. Knowledge has been referred to as a hierarchy of information wastebaskets. That is, part of the path to knowledge lies through sorting pieces of information and discarding the ones which are not relevant to a given situation so that the remaining pieces can be formed into a comprehensible pattern to inform decision-makers.

Effective leaders in industry, politics, and the military almost always rely on teams of aides who collect and organize information from both inside and outside the organization. We say that leaders who make unrealistic decisions through a lack of this kind of information processing have "lost touch," or that "they don't know the score."

The classroom can be a training ground for shared information processing, processing based on a trust in each member as a collaborator in gathering and sorting information. This kind of process training can also help young people to become more aware of their need for interdependence in accomplishing many of their own goals, and it can help them to form a realistic sense of what they can expect from different sorts of people, so that they can maintain a balance between unwisely trusting incompetent sources and being unwisely suspicious of helpful and competent sources.

One way to teach this kind of information processing is to ask the class to work in small problem-solving groups within the class. Whether it's a page of rate-time-distance problems, a series of sonnets from Shakespeare, or a sequence of lines from Vergil, groups of four or five students can work together and then make short reports or group lecturettes to the class.

If there are three important novels which represent a certain theme or period, then the class can be divided into three groups, each group asked to read one of the novels. Then, after reading the novels or at various stages during the reading process, the groups hold discussions about their novels. In each case the other members of the class listen to the discussion and ask questions.

Another possibility is for the teacher to ask the class, "What do you know, and what do you want to know?": For whatever the subject is (the pilgrims' first Thanksgiving, the anatomy of a frog, the concept of prejudice) the teacher asks the class to brainstorm all the things that they know about the subject, the teacher or volunteer students noting each item on the board. After four or five minutes, the teacher asks the students to reflect individually on what things they would like to know about the subject. Then after a minute or two for reflection, the teacher asks the students to say what some of the things they really want to know about the subject are. As the students volunteer, the teacher writes their questions down on the board.

When a list of ten or twelve questions has been gathered, there are a number of things that the class can do. The teacher may ask the class to look over the list of questions to see if there are any questions that individuals in the class might be able to answer or shed light on. This often produces some information from students who have special knowledge or insights in the field. Then the teacher might ask each student to choose one question that is most interesting to him. Those who have chosen the same question may form work groups or, perhaps, work independently. The questions can then form subjects for research and reports back to the class as a whole.

In asking "What do you know, and what do you want to know?" the teacher may find that certain pieces of misinformation appear among the items "known," but the teacher should write down every item which the students brainstorm, no matter how wrong or inaccurate it may be. There are several reasons for this: First, if the teacher serves as an instant arbiter of what shall and shall not be placed on the board, then some students may be reluctant to volunteer for fear of being put down. Second, it is important to know if misinformation does exist in the class, and to what extent it does exist. Third, many pieces of information may appear incorrect from the teacher's perspective but later become valid through supporting evidence from the students. Finally, this misinformation can be structured into a learning opportunity: At the end of the brainstorming, the teacher may ask the students to look over the list of things that they know and see if there are any items that they might disagree with. If disagreements arise, then each proponent may be asked to state his position, and the teacher can ask for some independent research.

For instance, suppose Mary notices that one of the items about Columbus is that he discovered America in 1491. She pipes up: "I think that's wrong; I think that it was 1492." Teacher: "How can we find out?" The lesson is thus expanded to include ways of finding and verifying information. On the other hand, if no one else questions the item, the teacher may say, "Hmmm—1491. The information that I remember is that the correct date was 1492. How can we find out who's right?"

If learning how to learn is one of the primary goals of formal education, then information processing—seeking, gathering, organizing, and sharing—is a vital skill. This is a skill that is little practiced in the traditional classroom where the teacher and his prescribed textbooks are viewed as the fountain of knowledge. Any activity or pattern of teaching that demonstrates the importance and effectiveness of collaboration in the processing of information is likely to increase the chances that the individual student can successfully cope with the real and ambiguous world of information outside the classroom.

IX:

VALUE EXPLORATION

AND CLARIFICATION

Take a pencil and write down four words that express the feelings that you have right now—don't wait, don't write sentences, just do it quickly.

Now that you have wrestled with your comfort and your commitment to continue reading this chapter, and now that you have chosen either to follow or not to follow the instructions in the first paragraph, let's see where an awareness of the here-and-now can lead:[1] It should come as no surprise that as human beings we are continually faced with choice situations: Shall I get up and get a pencil? Shall I bother to read further? Shall I grade papers this afternoon, or read a book, or go shopping, or . . . ? What should I do about my parents? Should I send some money to that cause that I say I believe in? And on and on and on.

Moreover, as teachers we see our students faced with a bewildering array of choice situations, choices

---

[1] This chapter is adapted from an article entitled "Values in the Classroom," which appeared in the *Independent School Bulletin*, October 1972.

concerning sex, family, friends, work, leisure, money, religion, time, goals, health, self-appraisal, death, and many more. And as the number of choices become over-powering, certain learning problems seem to arise: There is growing evidence that the problems of the under-achiever, the apathetic or inconsistent student, the drift-er, the over-conformer, the over-dissenter are often the result of a sense of alienation from one's own feelings, a lack of clarity in decision-making, a *confusion of values*.

Where are the guideposts to help in these choice situations? To what extent are the *shoulds* which we have given our young people through family, church, and school realistic to them, and what part of our young people's lives are spent in trying to reconcile those *shoulds* with the realities that they see? How can we help our young people to clarify their values so that they can make choices that are meaningful to them and congruent with their feelings as they perceive their world?

The object of this chapter is to present to teachers some considerations and activities that they can use to help students in their valuing process, not to introject or impose the teacher's values upon the student, but to help the student clarify his own feelings and values. A-long the way I hope that the reader will achieve a better understanding of himself and become more aware of his own valuing process, but it is no more necessary that a teacher should have a clearly defined value structure be-fore working with students on values than it is necessary for a football coach to be able to play all the positions better than the people on his team. Valuing is a con-tinuing process, and it is one of the conditions of exis-tence that teachers be groping with their own values as they teach others.

In talking about values in the classroom, I have

found it useful to divide the valuing process into six elements, four dealing with choosing, two with acting:[2]

CHOOSING:

1. **Identification of preferences:** What do I really like?

2. **Identification of influences:** What influences have led me to prefer this? How freely am I making my choice?

3. **Identification of alternatives:** What are the possible alternative choices? Have I given sufficient consideration to alternatives?

4. **Identification of consequences:** What are the probable and possible consequences for each alternative? Am I willing to risk the consequences? Are the consequences socially beneficial or socially harmful?

ACTING:

5. **Acting:** Am I able to act on this choice? Do my actions reflect the choice I have made?

6. **Patterning:** Does this choice represent a continuing commitment through action? How can I change the pattern of my life so that this choice is continually reflected in my actions?

These last two elements are very important because there is a great deal of evidence which indicates that a person's behavior does not necessarily correspond to his attitudes in a significant way. It is this lack of congruence which accounts for much of the personal dissatisfaction, anxiety, and apparent apathy which often characterize individuals who feel a lack of clarity in re-

---

[2] This is an adaptation by Robert C. Hawley and David D. Britton of the seven valuing criteria presented in Louis E. Raths, *et al, Values and Teaching* (Columbus, Ohio: Chas. E. Merrill Pub. Co., 1966).

lationship to society, who have a muddy valuing process.

Test, if you will, one of your values against these six elements: Write down very briefly a value you have connected with leisure time. I think, for instance, that I value hiking as a part of my life. I feel that I have chosen hiking freely, from among alternatives, and with a consideration of the consequences; I feel that hiking is one of my preferences; but when it comes to acting, I find that I have not done any hiking for more than a month, and there is no consistent pattern of hiking in my life. This is a significant finding for me. If I really value hiking, how must I change my life so that I can live closer to what I value? If I don't really value hiking, if I discover that there are other things that I value more highly, then perhaps I can feel less guilty about watching the football game on a brilliant Sunday afternoon. You can test any area that touches your life with these elements: How did you spend your last vacation, and how did you want to spend that vacation? How do you feel about war or pollution or race relations, and what are you doing about those feelings?

Here are three steps in helping others with the valuing process: The first step is to *open* the area—to stimulate a person to think about value-related areas and to encourage him to share his thoughts with others. As a teacher I feel that my tendency often used to be to divert the class away from value-related areas when I felt that they touched too closely to a person's life. What a waste! And how guilty I was of reinforcing the feelings of classroom artificiality by so doing! Perhaps the simplest way to encourage value exploration within the classroom is to stop the normal progress of the lesson when you feel that an important value area is being touched upon and to say, "Let's see how we can clarify this," or, "Let's deal with this."

The next step is to *accept* the thoughts, feelings, beliefs, and ideas of others non-judgmentally and encourage the others in the class to accept a person's feelings for what they are without trying to change them or criticizing them. This step helps the individual to know that he can be honest with others and with himself, no matter how negative or confused his feelings and ideas might be. And it is important always to respect his right to "pass," that is, to refuse to share his thoughts and feelings if he feels that the risks are too high. (Obviously it is important to help the individual to increase his level of risk-taking, but this is best done by acting in an open, honest, non-judgmental manner, rather than by attempting to force an issue).

And the third step is to *stimulate* additional thinking so that an individual can move towards a more comprehensive level of valuing. Here the emphasis should be kept on the individual, for it is only when an area touches and affects a person's life that he can really become involved in the valuing process. Going back to the six elements, here are some of the kinds of responses that can be helpful to an individual as he grapples with his values: What are the alternatives that you might consider? Where would this idea lead—what would the consequences be? Is this something that you have chosen freely, or is it something that you have been taught to believe? Is this something that you really prefer—do you value it? What actions has this led you to—is this something that you would like to do something about? Do you see any pattern of action in your life as a result of this—how would you like to change your life so that this would become a meaningful part?

It is important to use these clarifying questions sparingly and in a non-judgmental way. For instance, if a teacher sees a student pick up a snow ball and says, "Have you considered the consequences of that action?"

it does not matter how non-judgmental the teacher feels, the student, from long experience, will infer a criticism, a put-down. Or if I see my young son pulling his sister's hair, and I say, "Is this something that you really like to do?" he may very well burst into tears, feeling an implied chastisement.

The following are some specific techniques for value exploration and clarification. If possible, they should be done with others—members of your family or a small group of friends. See what kinds of discussion they bring and how they affect you. For many of these activities small discussion groups seem to work best. I like to divide a class into three- or four-person groups, using some random technique such as counting off by numbers so that people will move outside their immediate circle of friends. (Divide the number in the class by the number to be in each group, say thirty divided by three; then count off in tens and have all the ones group together, all the twos, etc.)

Value Voting:

With the class divided into small groups, the students vote on questions related to values. The teacher gives the following instructions: *To show agreement or positive feelings toward the question, raise your hand. If you feel very strongly in favor, wave your hand in the air. If you disagree or feel negative toward the question, turn your thumb down. For a very strong negative vote, thumb down and churning. If you have no feelings or wish to pass, arms folded.*

The teacher then asks a series of questions which involve value judgments. There should be no attempt to tally the vote. At the end of a few questions there should be a break to allow time for the members of the groups to share their feelings. They will probably wish to explore areas of disagreement and agreement with each other.

Sample Questions:
1. Would you try sky diving?
2. Would you tell someone he has bad breath?
3. Would you favor a more stringent dress code?
4. Would you like to try marijuana, at least once?
5. Do you think that the Apollo Program is a waste of our natural resources?
6. Would you carry a sign in a protest march?
7. Would you buy a vacation in Hawaii on credit?
8. Would you change your hairstyle if it meant earning 20 per cent more money?

Value voting can be useful for clarifying values in subject matter too:

History: Do you approve of John Brown's actions at Harper's Ferry?

English: Do you approve of Ma's actions in getting rid of Flag in *The Yearling?*

Science: Do you approve of vivisection?

In making up questions to vote on, the emphasis should be kept on the *you.* Action-oriented questions are good. And the questions should be taken from areas of real concern. Once they get the idea, the class will come up with relevant questions of their own, but it is important that everyone understand his right to pass if the questions seem too threatening.

Rank-Order:

Here participants are given three situations to rank as they perceive them, from best to worst, or, if they perceive them as all good (or bad), from most to least good (or bad). Rankings should be made individually. Then they may be compared and discussed with the others in the group. (It is possible, as with any of these activities, that the class will prefer to open the discussion to the class as a whole).

1. Rank these situations:

a. You are an Air Force bombadier about to drop bombs on suspected enemy troop concentrations, knowing that innocent civilians are likely to be killed and injured as well.

b. You are the executioner who must pull the switch on a convicted murderer in the electric chair.

c. You are a home-owner who is about to shoot at a dark moving shape which has entered your home at night.

After discussing your rank-orders, try the next:

2. If you were the principal of this school, rank these situations as to their desirability to you:

a. The students love you.

b. Your colleagues respect your opinion.

c. Your school is the showplace of the district.

After discussing your rank-ordering of these situations, try to expand this list by making up a situation that would be more desirable than the one you put at the top, and one that would be less desirable than your bottom-ranked situation. Now try ranking these:

3. As the parent of a seventeen-year-old daughter:

a. You discover that she has been sleeping with all the boys around—that she has the reputation of being promiscuous.

b. You receive a call from the police that she has been arrested for possession of marijuana.

c. She announces to you that she is engaged to marry a boy of another race.

After discussing your rankings, discuss how the list might change if it had been a seventeen-year-old son instead of daughter.

These three rank-orders all involve putting on another role. To that extent they give the individual a chance to get outside himself and glimpse the world from another's point of view. It is also useful to make up rank-orders that involve everyday choice situations for students:

4. Rank these actions that you might take when you see another student copying off your paper in a test:

a. Do nothing.

b. Hide your paper as well as you can with your arm, realizing that you cannot work as well in that position.

c. Call the teacher and ask if you can change your seat.

What other possibilities can you come up with?

5. A person in your class whom you don't like very well has been accused of taking some lunch money from the teacher's desk. You saw someone else take the money. How do you rank the following?

a. Take no action.

b. Defend the person openly, knowing that you will be pressured to tell who really took the money.

c. Write an anonymous letter to the principal explaining the situation without identifying the person.

What are some other possibilities? As with value voting, students can learn to make up rank-order situations to help clarify important issues in their own lives.

Here are some uses of rank-order problems in relation to traditional course content:

English: Rank Macbeth's motives for killing Duncan, from most powerful to least powerful:

a. To please his wife.

b. To gain power for himself.

c. To gain wealth.

d. To fulfill the prophecy of the witches.

History: Rank the following reasons that General Lee might have given for joining the Confederate rather than the Union Army:

a. To maintain slavery.

b. To assert the right of states to self-determination.

c. To defend his homeland.

d. To maintain his Southern life-style.

Math: Rank the following reasons for studying algebra in order of their importance to you:

a. Because it's a required course.

b. For future benefit—use in college.

c. For future benefit—use in my everyday life.

d. Training for my mind.

Forced-Choice Games:

Forced-choice games represent another type of activity designed to open the area of valuing and to stimulate additional thinking. It is important, as it is with any value exploration, to accept the feelings of the student openly and non-judgmentally, so that he can learn to become more open and direct about his feelings without the fear of reprisal or rebuke.

Space Ambassadors: [3]

Your group has been given the responsibility of selecting the five persons from the list of volunteer candidates below who are to be sent as the first representatives from the planet Earth to a planet in a distant galaxy which has been found to contain human life very similar to that on Earth. Do not worry about problems of time, space, language, life support, or surprise attack,

---

[3] Adapted from Robert C. Hawley & Isabel L. Hawley, *A Handbook of Personal Growth Activities for Classroom Use* (Amherst, Mass: Education Research Associates, 1972).

for modern technology has been able to take care of all of these. You will have fifteen minutes to reach a group decision. Try to avoid artificial decision-making such as voting or flipping coins.

The volunteers:

1. Assistant manager, New York bank, resident of Long Island, 39.

2. His wife, 37.

3. Welfare recipient, mother of six, Puerto Rican, 32.

4. Head of local construction firm, son of Italian immigrant, 48.

5. Catholic priest, white, 28.

6. Editor of large college daily newspaper, 20.

7. Career Army officer, major, Vietnam veteran, 46.

8. Model for television commercials, male, 49.

9. High school drop-out, working in neighborhood youth center, 18.

10. President, New England Chapter, World Federalists, female, 68.

11. Artist, involved with group marriage, pictures in leading national magazine, 41.

12. His younger wife, writer of unpublished children's stories, 19.

13. His older wife, M.D., just published major research on cancer, 47.

14. Chief, Black-fox tribe, Chena American Indians, 87.

15. Principal, urban elementary school, white, 43.

It would be nice if there were more data available on these candidates, but you must remember that in the real world we are continually forced to make judgments based upon incomplete data.

After your committee has reached its decision, discuss what values you hope the chosen group will communicate.

Forced-choice games can be fun to make up, and you can suit the material to the age that you are working with. For young children, for instance, you could make up a Noah's Ark game: Which five or six pairs of animals would you choose to put in the ark, and what are the characteristics of those animals that you admire? Or a desert island game could force a choice about characters, or electrical appliances, or five things that are in the person's room. The important thing is to open the area of what a person values, and to stimulate him to think why he values it.

Value Whips:

Here is an activity that can be used without breaking the class into smaller groups. It consists of having each person in turn share his feelings and ideas about a given topic: for instance, "The time I felt closest to nature this week was . . ," or "The high point of my week was . . ." As the whip moves from person to person around the room, there is often a growing awareness of the commonality of man, as well as of the varieties of experience. Sometimes a whip can give a person new ideas about how he can change his life or add new skills to his repertoire. As each student examines himself and articulates his feelings, he comes to know himself better, and to begin to own and value his feelings for what they are. If a whip topic touches too closely upon a person's life, and if he is not prepared to move to that level of risk-taking, he can pass. And the teacher should not be afraid to include himself in the whip.

Here are some other possible whips: "The thing that disturbed me most this week was . . ."; "The time I had the most fun with children this week was . . ."; "The

time I had the most fun with adults this week was . . .";
"I wonder . . ."; "The new skill that I learned this summer that I am proud of is . . ."; "I am proud that I have
helped race relations by . . ."; "I am proud that I struck
a blow against pollution by . . ."; "I wish . . . ."

A whip is a good way to start a class, or to end a
class. It lets the students know that their feelings are
important and that it is proper to deal with their feelings in the classroom.

Value Cards:

Ask the students to bring in a three-by-five card
once a week on which they have composed, as well as
they know how, a statement about what they value. The
card can be prose or a poem, or a picture, or a collage,
any statement of value to the person. The card will not
be graded in any way, but the teacher will read two or
three cards each day, anonymously unless the author
wishes to reveal himself. On some days the class could
be asked to comment, on others not. I suspect most
teachers would be surprised at how much poetry, how
much feeling, how much openness, comes out of a weekly value card. At the end of the term the cards can be
passed back to the students so that they can see how
they have progressed in valuing.

"I Learned . . ." Statements:

At the end of a discussion about values or after
one of the other activities, it can be clarifying to ask for
some *"I Learned . . ." Statements*. It is generally better
not to use a whip for "I Learned . . ." Statements but to
let anyone who wants to share speak out. In framing an
"I Learned . . ." Statement the emphasis is on what one
has learned about himself. Every "I Learned . . ." Statement should have two *I*'s: "I learned that *I* . . ."; "I re-
learned that *I* . . ."; "I noticed that *I* . . ."; "I re-affirmed
that *I* . . ." It is important to keep the focus on what a
person has learned about himself. Some "I learned a-

bout something else" statements will slip by, but the closer the group can be kept to the second *I*, the more each participant will learn about his own feelings and values. For example, if a student says, "I learned that all people are different," it is probably not as helpful to him as if he had said, "I learned that I often forget how different people are."

Here-and-Now Words:

We spend so much of our lives in a silent compact to avoid confronting the here-and-now, that it seems at first strange, unnatural, to express our here-and-now feelings, even to ourselves. And yet if we are to work at determining what we value, our here-and-now feelings are absolutely essential. At the beginning of this chapter I asked you to write down four feelings that you had just at that time. I would like you to do that again now:

Write the date and the exact time, and then write four words or brief phrases that describe feelings that you have right here and now. Then take one of those four items and write two sentences expanding that feeling.

Here-and-now words are private messages to one's self, an attempt to get in touch with what is really going on inside the self. I generally feel reluctant to ask for volunteers to share their here-and-now words with the class, but if and when a class develops the openness and positiveness and the ability to give non-judgmental feedback which are essential ingredients in the process of self-awareness, then the sharing of here-and-now words can be a significant clarifying technique.

In addition to the immediate self-awareness that here-and-now words can bring, by comparing here-and-now words collected over a period of time and from different situations, an individual can gain insight into patterns of feelings and behaviors that are important to him. The teacher might, for instance, ask each member of a class to write here-and-now words at a given time each day for two weeks, or once a week for a term, or each waking hour for one day, and then to assemble his here-and-now words and see what patterns of feeling run through the current of his life.

If you did write the here-and-now words at the beginning of this chapter, then you might stop now and compare them with the ones you have just written. If you did not, then try to think what were the voices that were going through your mind when you were asked to examine your here-and-now.

If we continue to think of today's problems in terms of yesterday's feelings surely we will go the way of the dinosaurs. The valuing process is part of the process of becoming, of living. As we continue to grow and change, as we continue to receive and process new data from the external world, so our values must grow and change. It is through the process of continual self-discovery that we avoid closing our minds to the constantly changing realities of the world around us. Perhaps the most important awareness that we can help our students with is the awareness of the growing, changing, becoming quality of life, and of the need to listen to the new voices that are within us each new day and each new hour.

NOTE: For additional value-clarifying activities see the following, listed in more detail in Appendix A:

Raths, Harmin, & Simon, *Values and Teaching.*

Simon, Howe, & Kirschenbaum, *Values Clarification: A Handbook of Practical Strategies.*

Simon, Hawley, & Britton, *Composition for Personal Growth: Values Clarification Through Writing.*

Hawley & Hawley, *A Handbook of Personal Growth Activities for Classroom Use.*

X:

PLANNING FOR CHANGE

It's not a question of whether or not to change, but whether or not we can control the way we are changing. We are living in an *Alice in Wonderland* world where you have to run just to stay where you are. To get anywhere you have to run even faster than that. The pieces on the chess board keep changing and the rules are never the same. When we stop and try to remember and enforce the old rules, we get swept back into the past, lose contact with the here-and-now. Since we do not perceive the new realities, we become unable to change our behaviors to cope with the demands of the external world, and our chances of survival as a society are severely reduced.

The previous chapters have dealt, at least in part, with seeing the world as a continually changing process rather than as a series of fixed and predetermined categories. This chapter will explore what we can do to survive in the changing world.

The following is one possible pattern of altering our behavior to meet the new and constantly changing demands of new realities: First, identify alternative courses of action. The more different alternatives we can find, the more likely it is that there will be one or a combination of several that will work for us. Second, identify resources. This increases the range of alternatives and expands the list of the possible choices among them. The richer the reservoir of available resources, the more likely that satisfactory solutions can be found. Third, decide. This implies a conscious effort to make a choice rather than to allow the flow of time to make the decision for us. Finally, find ways to act on the decision. As those who have given up smoking several times know, failure to change is often the result of an inability to act on decisions rather than an inability to decide.

Generating Alternatives

How do you send love to someone far away? Send a card? Write a letter? Telephone? Telegraph flowers? This question is one that I often use to introduce the technique of brainstorming as a means of generating useful alternatives. Under the strict rules of brainstorming groups have been able to come up with as many as sixty different ways to send love to someone far away, and they have done it in only four or five minutes. Of course, some of the ways are probably not practicable, such as sky writing, a television commercial, sending your toenail clippings, ESP, for example. But others may be means that some can employ at least some of the time: Send your children, agree to watch the same TV show at the same time and think of each other, place an ad in their local newspaper, place their name on a free sample or junk mail list, and I've heard of more than one instance where a person has had a billboard erected telling of his love. The point is that we frequently work within fairly narrow ranges of alternatives—mostly we send cards, sometimes we call, occasionally we send flowers, and that's about the extent of the alternatives that we use. For Christmas in 1972 over two and one-half billion cards were sent through the public mails in the United States. There's nothing wrong with Christmas cards, but this is an indication to me that we tend to think and act within a much narrower range of alternatives than need be.

Probably the most effective method for generating alternatives is brainstorming. Brainstorming is designed to produce a large body of data which can later be worked on and refined. Here are the rules: First, there is to be no negative evaluation of any idea proposed during the brainstorming period. When we start to evaluate ideas one by one, we slow down the flow and begin to narrow our range to those that we feel sure may be workable. Second, work for quantity. The more ideas expressed during the brainstorming period the better. This rule tends to reinforce the no evaluation rule. Third, work for zany, far-out ideas. We mostly know the practical ideas; it is often from the unusual and unrealistic ideas that the germ for a new solution arises. Fourth, try to piggy-back or springboard off another idea where possible. Often we refrain from adding to or changing an idea because it belongs to someone else. In brainstorming, the focus is on solving the problem rather than on giving individual credit for ideas: One person's unrealistic idea may spark a practical idea from someone else. Fifth, record each idea. This underscores the notion of no negative evaluation of ideas. If we stop to decide which ideas we will record and which we will skip over, then we have made an evaluation. Also, the entire list may be useful after the brainstorming period is over, as we review the list looking for those ideas that we can modify into a practical solution. Finally, set a time limit for the brainstorming period and keep to it. We are capable of deferring our evaluation for only so long. If there is no announced ending time, then we start evaluating our ideas to try to judge when we have enough to work with, and this pushes us toward working for quality rather than quantity. Depending on the problem, five to ten minutes is generally adequate for the brainstorming period.

After the brainstorming period, the list should be

read over or displayed so that all can see it. Then the group can begin to work on a final solution from the position of having a great deal of common data. Or if the problem is the concern of a single individual, then he can collect the lists and work on his solution in private, carrying with him a rich bank of possible alternatives.

THE RULES OF BRAINSTORMING
1. **No negative evaluation.**
2. **Work for quantity, not quality.**
3. **Work for zany, far-out ideas.**
4. **Work to piggy-back or springboard off each other's ideas.**
5. **Record each idea.**
6. **Set and keep a strict time limit.**

Groups and individuals who practiced brainstorming often fall into the practice of informal brainstorming even when they have not formally determined to brainstorm a problem. This informal, creative way of thinking can help to turn cooperative ventures from a climate of secret competition to one of active collaboration and support.

Identifying Resources

The key to discovering new resources is in looking at the world from a new angle. Most discoveries are really made up of pieces that have been available all along and are suddenly seen in a new relationship to one another or to the problem. We are just beginning to tap the great reserve of teaching potential that comes through peer teaching and cross-age helping, for instance. These are great resources that were structured out of existence by efficiency methods of education— grade levels, homogeneous groupings, division of college-bound and vocational schools, for instance.

Another great resource is the community. Seen formerly as a place for field-trips, frilly extras, the community setting is now beginning to offer to some students a reason to stay in school, a rationale for learning to read and add, etc. Furthermore, the community is full of individuals who possess special skills and knowledge which they are eager to share with others. Parents, older brothers and sisters, friends, and many professional and business people are often willing to give their time and are delighted to be asked to share their special experiences.

For instance, suppose that Sally, a high school sophomore, checks out of school in the middle of the morning to show her younger brother's fifth grade class her slides of Canada or her special way of knitting scarves. Image the self-esteem that Sally gains, the respect that her brother gains for her, and the new insights that the fifth graders gain from this resource. Jenny's mother comes in to help the children make cookies in the third grade: why can't Bill's father come in to talk to the eleventh grade about financing a car?

What are the other resources close at hand? Look at the school office, the cafeteria, the kitchen, the furnace room. Why can't the students poll the kitchen staff, asking for their ranking of three important issues in a forthcoming election, or find out how much fuel the building consumes per day and determine the per pupil cost of heating the building, or do a time and motion study of the school principal?

Another potential source of educational materials is the wastebasket. What do we regularly throw away that could be useful? Popsicle sticks? Styrofoam cups? Computer print-out paper? Egg cartons? The list goes on and on. Start with the material and force-fit an educational use. How can I use popsicle sticks in English class?—Write a vocabulary word on each one, put them in a big tin can, shake them about, and ask each student to draw one, etc., etc. How can I use computer print-out in history class?—Have the students make a time line of events in the Civil War and another of events in the Vietnam War, then display the two charts one above the other.

Many of these proposals represent a kind of backward planning. That is, we start with a resource, try to look at it from a new angle and see what crazy schemes we can have for it, and only then decide whether or not the schemes that we come up with fit some of our educational goals. This represents a deliberate deferring of evaluation while we are identifying new resources. All too often when we establish an objective, our thinking becomes ultra-rational, and we limit ourselves to the boundaries of the known. This kind of backwards planning opens up a whole new range of creative resources. One word of caution is necessary, however. There's no point in having the students count the cars on the street or make masks out of egg cartons just because these resources are available. Only when these activities can be seen as learning opportunities which match the objectives of the class can they be included as a legitimate part of the school day.

Decision-Making

No matter how objective the criteria seem to be, decisions are always based on value judgments. Take admissions to college, for example: If the decision-makers, admissions officials in this case, decide to use strictly objective measurements such as College Entrance Examination Board test scores and grade-point averages from applicants' high schools, then they are placing a positive value on these measurements as opposed to other criteria that they could use (principal's recommendation, interview, autobiographical letter, color of eyes, length of hair, etc.). The admissions officers may choose these criteria because they believe that these criteria will select the type of person that they desire as students, or because these are the only feasible criteria to process under the pressures of time and resources, or because these are the criteria that have "always been used." Whatever the reasons are for selecting a particular set of criteria, the fact remains that the decision is based on value judgments, either conscious or unconscious.

The same is true when I buy a car. My decision may be based on objective criteria such as price, mechanical performance, and style, but when I select these as criteria I am placing a value on money, dependability, speed, cornering, and so forth. There is no decision which is not founded on value judgment.

If all decisions are based on value-related criteria, then two implications follow: First, effective decision-making is more likely to take place when the values underlying the available options are explored and clarified. Second, decisions will serve the decider better when the criteria that he uses are based on an awareness and understanding of the end goals of the decision.

In the case of the admissions officers, if the end goal of the admissions procedure is to select students who are capable of doing the academic work of the college, then those criteria which best determine who is academically capable are appropriate. If, on the other hand, the end goal of the admissions officers is to find those persons who can best use the college experience to promote their own social-self-actualization so that they will become a social force for the amelioration of society, then another set of criteria may be more appropriate than the College Board scores.

Similarly, if my end goal for a new car is to provide reliable, comfortable transportation, then my criteria for decision-making may be quite different than if my end goal is to get transportation as cheaply as possible or if my end goal is to enhance my self-image and my feelings of prestige and worthiness in the eyes of my peers.

There is a third important element in effective decision-making: the identification of creative alternatives. Any time that a problem is close and persistent, it is easy to get locked into a narrow range of options. For instance, when we were shopping for an automobile recently, we felt that one of the essential requirements was more space for our growing family. We also wanted something that was small for city driving and economical on gas. At some point in our deliberations we seemed to get locked into thinking only of new compact imported station wagons. We looked at many varieties but didn't seem to find the one that was right for us. Tired and frustrated, we decided to put off the job of getting a new car for a month or two. During that hiatus we had a chance to explore some of our values. Did it have to be new? Imported? A station wagon? And what were all the things we wanted the car to do? When we went back to shopping seriously, we quickly homed in on the right car for us: a new, imported, medium-sized, two-door sedan with a very large trunk. We had gotten away from the problem enough to break our narrow, locked-in pattern of thinking, and we had given ourselves a chance to clarify just what the end goals of buying a car were for us.

Formal decision-making can be seen as a four-step process: First identify the end goals of the decision and rank them in order of importance to the decision-maker. Second, list all available options, including wild, unrealistic ideas wherever possible because these far-out ideas often contain the germ of some new creative and workable option. Third, examine the value of each of the options. What are its benefits, what are its weaknesses? Finally, match the values of each option with the end goals. Which options seem likely to lead most directly to the end goals? Is there a creative blend of options which can serve the end goals better than the options as listed?

Of course, most decisions are not made as a result of such formal deliberations. The important things are an awareness of the end goals and a realization of the power of seeking creative options to meet those end goals. One way that this can be tackled in the classroom is through decision-charting.

For this process the blackboard is divided into three columns. The first column is labeled *End Goals*, the second *Options*, and the third *Option Values*. Then a decision area is selected for study: to buy a car, to choose what to do after high school, to choose a course of study, etc. Then the students brainstorm possible end goals of that decision area, with the teacher recording items on the board in the first column. Then students are asked to rank the end goals in order of importance to them, first individually and then as a group. Next, the class brainstorms a list of options that might be available for the decision. Those options that seem most useful are then selected for further work, and for each one the values inherent in the option are listed. Now the decision-makers have before them a great quantity of information organized in a meaningful fashion. By comparing the option values with the important end goals, they can determine which of the available options is likely to prove most appropriate (See Table A).

Another graphic way to look at decision-making is the force-field analysis. When an either-or decision is to be faced, such as going to college or getting a job,

Table A:
DECISION-CHARTING

Decision: *Buying a Car*

Ranking	End Goals	Options	Option Values
1	*transportation*	*economy car*	*money, parking*
2	*fun*	*sports car*	*impress others*
			have fun
4	*feeling of importance*		
5	*to impress others*	*fix up junked car*	*fun to do*
3	*make money with*	*station wagon*	*use to carry stuff*
	etc.	*etc.*	*etc.*

quitting smoking or continuing smoking, buying a record or putting the money in a savings account, etc., then the problem can be looked at as a field of opposing forces, some pulling in one direction, some in the other. The blackboard is divided into two columns, each labeled with one of the two choices. Then the class brainstorms all the forces pulling in one direction, the teacher recording each item. Next the class brainstorms all the forces pulling in the other direction, and the teacher records these on the board in the other column. Now the students can rank the two lists of forces in order of strength (or importance). Once again a quantity of the information which affects the decision has been organized and displayed in a useful way (See Table B).

One final tool in teaching decision-making is role-playing. In a short role-play two persons can try to convince each other of the value of going to college on one hand or getting a job on the other. Or one person can play both roles, moving back and forth between two chairs, one marked *to quit smoking* and the other *not to quit smoking*. For a third kind of role-playing two chairs are set out, one representing Cautious Bill, the

Table B:
FORCE-FIELD ANALYSIS

Decision: *Smoking*

Forces compelling me to continue	Forces compelling me to give it up
taste	*health*
use in social situations	*parents*
makes me feel grown up	*cost*
keeps mosquitoes away in summer	*can't taste as well*
keeps my weight down	*smells up my clothes*
etc.	*etc.*

other Adventurous Bill. The two chairs carry on a dialogue about whether Bill should spend the summer at home cutting grass and earning money or hitchhike across the country. The members of the class are divided in half, one group supplying the dialogue for Cautious Bill, the other half for Adventurous Bill. These role-plays can provide a great deal of useful data. They are most effective when followed by a discussion and analysis which focuses on both the specific decisions involved and the decision-making process.

Decision-charting, force-field analysis, and role-playing are ways to foster an awareness of the decision-making process. These are teaching tools which are useful in developing concepts such as *opposing forces* and *end goals*. It is probably unrealistic to expect that many students will begin to make formal decision charts or force-field charts or engage in role-playing when facing important decisions, but when young people are more aware of the forces that shape their decisions and of the end goals that their decisions point toward, then they may be able to make more effective decisions for themselves and for the society that they will create.

Acting on Decisions

It's easy to decide—what's hard is acting on those decisions. I've decided to take up jogging several times. Old habits are hard to break. Established relationships work towards self-preservation. Patterns of behavior become so interlocking that any alteration is likely to lead to such a general uneasiness that the new change cannot be tolerated.

For instance, take the area of curriculum development. One of the reasons that curricular reform has been so unsuccessful is that we can't seem to get rid of the old patterns, old relationships, old habits. We think in terms of pre-established categories—English, math, history, and so on; and we find ourselves unable to break those categories. Nothing much has been changed in the secondary school curriculum: Instead we have tried to add things—sex education, drug education, driver education, group counseling. We tuck all these new and important additions to the curriculum into the cracks and corners of an already overstuffed day.

We've made enough decisions about what we *do* need to teach. What we need to do is make some hard decisions about what *not* to teach, what to pull out of the curriculum so that it is once again comprehensible. The same is true of our personal lives. I feel myself getting flabby, muscle-tone going out as I sit at my typewriter exercising only my fingers. But by the time I'm finished with my day, I'm too tired for exercises, and I can't seem to do them when I get up (The children have to be gotten off to school.), and in between, the day is full already. If I'm serious about adopting a daily exercise routine (which apparently I'm not), then I have to decide what it is that I'm doing now that I can eliminate from my daily schedule or else find a way to do two things at once.

The second part of acting on decisions is sticking with the new decision long enough for it to become established as a new pattern of behavior. For personal behaviors Matthew Maltz in *Psychocybernetics* suggests that about three weeks are required for a new pattern of behavior to become established. So if you are quitting smoking, try to last for a three-week period, counting the days. It may get easier after that. For more complex changes the period of adjustment may be longer. The New York City School System is said to have tried every educational reform in existence—for one week. When the reform didn't produce results in the short run, it was rejected. Eliminate grades, and you may have parents and students on your back for a whole year, maybe two. Significant change, radical change needs time to become established.

PART THREE:
NOTES ON TEACHING FOR PERSONAL
AND SOCIAL GROWTH

XI:
POSITIVE FOCUS

If you ask a teenager to list his personal strengths on one side of a page and then turn the paper over and list his personal weaknesses on the other, chances are that he will come up with about six items on the strengths side, but that he'll write on and on and even ask for more paper on the weakness side—listing about seven times as many weaknesses as strengths.[1] Our culture is so heavily over-balanced toward focusing on the negative, on weaknesses, on what we can't do, that there is little time left to build on the positive, on our strengths, on what we *can* do. And the average class-room is no exception, reflecting the focus of the larger culture not only in the attitude of the students and of the teacher, but in the way that students relate to one another and in the way that the students relate to the teacher and to the school. One of the questions that I am most often asked by teachers is, "How can I make my classroom a positive, growth-enhancing place when

---

[1]Unpublished study conducted by Dr. Herbert Otto.

my students and I habitually focus on weaknesses, where the climate of the larger community is so hostile?"

Furthermore, we learn very early that it is bad manners to show too much praise or admiration for others, and it is absolutely in the worst of taste to take pride in or even to acknowledge our own accomplishments and strengths. The person who goes out of his way to praise or affirm the strengths of others is considered "unrealistic," a "Pollyanna," or a "brown-noser." The person who takes pride in his accomplishments or affirms his strengths is known as conceited, boastful, stuck-on-himself. We prefer understatement to praise, modesty to self-affirmation. And yet in maintaining this culturally acceptable facade we drain our own personal energy and reduce the energy of others so that there is a diminished amount of energy available for constructive social action.

In an experiment designed to show the effect of positive and negative personal feedback,[2] a class at a major eastern university was rigged so that the students, about twenty in a graduate history section, had special instructions. The professor was unaware of the experiment or of the fact that he was being video-taped by a concealed camera. At the beginning of the tape the professor is lecturing, head down, hands grasping the lectern, reading from his notes in a monotone. The students are sprawled in various postures of inattention and boredom. At a given moment the students start to act more interested in the lecture—they sit up, nod their heads, smile, lean forward, and give other non-verbal signs of interest and support. Like a flower unfolding,

---

[2] Described to me by Dr. David D. Britton, to whom I am indebted for introducing me to the notion of positive focus and to much of the material in this chapter.

the professor moves away from the podium, begins to use his hands in expressive gestures, speaks more energetically, develops eye contact with members of the class, and has become a more lively and interesting speaker. He grows and blossoms under conditions of positive relationship with his class. The experiment continues, however, as, on a clandestine signal, the students return to their original postures of boredom and inattention. In less than three minutes the professor is back behind the safety of his desk, hands clenching the lectern, droning on from his lecture notes, a withered shadow of the person that had been. This is what we can do for each other: We can enhance each other's lives, build on each other's strengths, or we can tear each other down, enervate and cripple.

Teachers are seemingly forced into the role of providing negative focus. Grading compositions, correcting tests, marking off for spelling, diagnosing reading problems all have a distinctly negative focus, and I am convinced that these practices are at least as damaging as they may be beneficial. Not only do these negative-focus teacher behaviors diminish the students' feelings of self-esteem, but also where a teacher identifies a learning deficiency such as a "spelling problem" or a "calculating problem" or a "reading problem," then this labeling in effect gives the student permission to allow that "problem" to continue until the teacher does something about it. The "problem" becomes the teacher's and there is a subtle shift of responsibility for learning from the student to the teacher. (I suspect that this is one reason that remedial reading programs have in general been so abysmally ineffective: When he is classed as a "remedial reader," the student realizes that he has a special problem about which he really can do nothing without the help of an expert. The problem of dyslexia will not be resolved until it is seen as one aspect of a larger problem which also includes a lack of self-respect, feelings of powerlessness, etc.).

Grades foster a negative focus. Even an *A minus* is a sign of negativity. Points are always taken *off*. I know an English teacher who would have given Shakespeare only 98 for *Hamlet* because, after all, no one is perfect. Standardized testing is another school institution that often focuses on the negative: Did you realize that half of the school population is only average or below on any given standardized achievement test? A third generally negative focus in the school situation is the use of comments instead of or in addition to grades. Teachers almost always feel that they must make a balanced comment, stressing both the strengths and the weaknesses of the student. (In fact, many parents would question the teacher's ability if the comment sheet showed only positive comments). But given a page divided equally between positive and negative comments, many people will see only the negative ones. Any attempt to maintain a "realistic" focus on both negative and positive ultimately winds up focusing strongly on the negative.

But to return to the problem: How can we build a classroom climate that is positive and growth-enhancing? How can we and our students learn to identify and build on our own strengths and the strengths of others? I see two stages—first to foster an awareness of the general negative focus to the degree that it exists; and second to develop skills in positive focus.

One useful technique for the awareness stage is brainstorming. The class can be asked to brainstorm for five minutes all the things that students can do to each other and that teachers can do to students that get students down or create feelings of defensiveness in them. Then another five minutes are spent brainstorming all the things that students can do that raise feelings of self-esteem and supportiveness. A general discussion can follow, focusing on how to change so that the class becomes more supportive of each other. Another possibility is to ask the students to brainstorm all the self-put-downs that they can think of—that is, all the things that they can say and think about themselves that make them feel less worthy. And then they should brainstorm all the things that students can think about themselves to make themselves feel more powerful, more worthy. This can be followed by a discussion of why we put ourselves down so much and how we can change.

For the second stage, developing skills in positive focus, perhaps the first thing is to stress that positive focus can be considered a skill, and just as in learning a new game, like tennis for instance, no one is expected to be perfect at first. We can accept our sometimes clumsy attempts to give each other positive feedback because we are, after all, learning a new skill. A second step is to ask the students to monitor their own self-put-downs and to try to change to statements of self-affirmation. Students can try to catch each other at self-put-downs: "I'm hearing you putting yourself down. That's against the rules in this class." And as a forfeit, when a student is caught putting himself down, he must frame a statement of self-affirmation. The other students can help: "I caught you putting yourself down; now you have to make a self-affirming statement. I like the way you smile; I like the way you listen; I like the way you stand up for what you think is right—How about one of those?"

A third way to practice skills in positive focus is for the teacher to call for a validating round.[3] Validat-

---

[3] This activity owes its inspiration to Sidney B. Simon's elaboration on the validating principles in Harvey Jackman's re-evaluation counseling technique.

ing rounds generally come at the end of small group discussions of personal topics such as "My happiest moment from early childhood," or "The one day I would like to live over again because it was just about perfect," or "If I could do anything I wanted to for two whole days, I'd . . ." Or the validating round can occur after the students have read their compositions to each other in small groups or tried to reach consensus on a forced-choice problem, etc. To begin the validating round, each person writes the name of each of the other persons in the small group, skipping four lines between names. (Generally this activity works best when the class is divided into groups of four or five). Then the teacher asks the students to write two positive statements about each of the other students in the group, being as specific as possible, and using, if they wish, some of the following sentence starters: *I like the way you . . .* or *You're a lot like me when you . . .* or *It made me feel good when you said . . .* or *You are . . . .*

The teacher should remind the students that this is a skill-building exercise: It's probably going to feel uncomfortable reading each of your validating statements, and it most likely will seem embarrassing to hear them read to you; but this is practice in both giving and receiving positive feedback, so do the best you can, and remember that we can all make allowance for not being perfect at a new skill.

Then the teacher asks that in each group the students focus on one person at a time and everybody read his validating statements about that one person. Then the focus moves to the next person, and so on around the group. *Caution:* It is important to allow enough time to complete this activity within the class period. Generally twenty minutes is enough for a group of four, especially if the teacher warns the class of the time five minutes before the bell. If there is not enough time for the validating round, it is better to postpone it until the start of the next day's class.

Positive focus requires practice and faith. It is not easy to go counter to the general norms of our culture and the beliefs and attitudes of so many of our fellow humans. But over time, a continuing and steadfast focus on the positive in life, on our strengths, and on the strengths of others can help to restore in our students their personal energy, their feelings of power, their sense of worth so that they can see themselves as positive forces who can contribute to the task of building a better world.

XII:
GRADES AND EVALUATION

Fantasy: It's payday, and the workers are standing around the cashier's office talking in small groups. Smith goes up to the window, gets his pay envelope, rips it open eagerly and exclaims: "A two hundred dollars! Wow, I really hit it this week! Boy, did I fool that old bat. Hey, Brown, how much did you get?" Brown looks at him sullenly, "A twenty-eight dollars. That bastard had it in for me this week. I couldn't do anything right for her." Smith grins: "It's not what you do, it's how you do it. Give her a little of the old brown nose like I do."

Suppose just for an instant that people in real life were graded just like kids in school and paid accordingly. The boss keeps her idea of how much you should get in a little black book full of letters and numbers. She averages the number of fenders that you were able to put on during the test period with your score on the welding proficiency test (WPT), adds in the scores that she pulled out of the air for the three times that she called on you to check your work, and throws in an attitude grade and perhaps something for effort. Then she adds it all up, averages it, and converts it to dollars of pay. If you don't think it was fair, you can always complain to the supervisor, but it's his job to back her up, and he always does.

I would expect that if people in the real world were graded like kids in school, we would see an alarming jump in the number of assaults, murders, suicides, and divorces per year. Grades just aren't very fair, and the wonder of it is that students put up with them as peaceably as they do.

The litany against grading is long and well-rehearsed.[1] The following is a brief synopsis of my reasons for wanting the grading system abolished:

1. Grades are quixotic—not tied to reality. *Some* test scores are reliable measures which are valid for measuring *some* specific things. But the practice of using a variety of unreliable measures to begin with (grades on homework, tests, compositions, class participation, effort), then weighting those measures according to the teacher's hunch (tests count two-thirds, homework one-sixth, effort and class participation one-sixth, etc.), and finally giving a comprehensive score for "English" or "Math" or whatever, produces a score that is of doubtful validity as a measure of anything.

2. Grades shift the locus of evaluation from the person himself to an external agency. We are becoming a race of other-directed creatures, motivated by what we feel others want and are looking for. Shifting the locus of evaluation from internal to external erodes our creativity and our self-motivation. Although others, including the teacher, provide a valuable source of feedback as the individual shapes his life, if we want creative, self-motivated, self-directed people, we must steadfastly refuse to use procedures which corrupt that internal locus of evaluation, the organismic feeling that this is good and right for me not because someone else says so but because my guts and my brain tell me so.

---

[1] See for example, the following: Kirschenbaum, Simon, & Napier, *Wad-Ja-Get? The Grading Game in American Education* (New York: Hart Publishing Co., 1971). William Glasser, *Schools Without Failure* (New York: Harper & Row, 1969).

3. Grades extinguish internal motivation. There is clear evidence that external rewards and punishments shift the locus of motivation from the intrinsic reward of doing a worthwhile task well to the external motivation of gaining a reward or avoiding a penalty. In a controlled study one group of students was given a set of puzzle blocks, which most people would consider intrinsically interesting, and paid a sum of money for each correct solution. The other group was given the same blocks and asked to do the same puzzles. In the "rest period" after each group had done its work, the group which had not been paid continued to work on the puzzle, finding new and intriguing solutions. The group which had been paid showed little interest in the blocks now that they were not being paid to work on them. Clearly the intrinsic motivation, the natural curiosity and delight in discovery, had been extinguished in the paid group.

When we pay our students with grades, we do much the same thing. It is worthwhile to note, however, that praise does not have the same effect as money. Another group of students, in the experiment above, who were given verbal rewards ("That's very good," "You did that one very well," etc.) showed the same continuing interest in the blocks as the group which got no reward or money. In contrast to the notion, expressed by many people, that praise has the same effect as tangible reward, apparently this verbal praise acts as feedback which increases self-esteem and reinforces internal motivation.

4. Grades shift the responsibility for learning from the student to the teacher. With the emphasis on grades, the student is motivated toward getting a good grade rather than toward learning something. It becomes the teacher's responsibility to structure the curriculum so that those things that the student does to get a good grade are also the things that the student should be do-

ing in order to learn. This places a double burden on the teacher of both diagnosing the learning needs of the student and also finding ways of structuring graded learning opportunities to fill those needs. And the student is left with the generally unproductive job of figuring out what he should be doing in order to get a good grade rather than what he should be doing in order to learn.

5. Grades shift the role of the teacher from helper to judge. How much will you trust your lawyer if you know that he is also your only jury? To what extent does this limit your ability to confide in him? To what extent does it motivate you toward buttering him up rather than being honest with him?

6. Grades debase potentially meaningful work, taint that which might be real and exciting with the odor of an academic exercise. For example, one way to let students engage in meaningful writing for potentially responsive audiences is to encourage letter writing. But if the letter must be shown to the teacher to be checked over for spelling, mechanics, and style (A grade is implicit in this process even though it may not show in the teacher's book.), then instead of being a real letter to a real Bobby Orr, Raquel Welch, or Senator Church, it becomes an exercise for English class, an exercise which is then incidentally sent on to someone else. A sort of inverse proof of this point is that the things we don't grade become unimportant in the students' eyes. We don't grade original poetry ("How can you grade a poem?") and so the writing of poetry becomes unimportant ("I scribbled something down and then spent extra time on my math because we were getting a grade on that."). Art and music are seldom graded and are traditionally considered to be the "frills" of education.

7. Grading narrows the focus of teaching concerns to those things which can be easily graded. This is prob-

ably the reason that so much grammar is taught and that math is taught as a series of problems requiring solutions. Grading leads teachers to teach those things which can be graded (multiplication facts, comma rules, causes of the Civil War, second conjugation verbs, etc.) rather than those that defy grades (ethics, logic, ability to empathize, collaboration, self-motivation, etc.). It is characteristic of many schools today to have a statement of purpose which reflects the ideals of teaching for personal and social growth but to have a curriculum in which that kind of teaching is unlikely to occur.

8. Finally, grades foster a competitive, win-lose atmosphere, where students see each other not as possible resources and collaborators, but as competitors for the same prize. When students wave their hands eagerly to answer the teacher's question, it is often not because they want to share an insight with the class but because they want to have the teacher recognize their superiority. They want to say it first. (For those who argue that competition is healthy, it's the American way, where would we be now if we didn't have competition, doesn't noncompetition lead to mediocrity, etc., I answer that competition is so pervasive, so ingrained in our society, that there is no need to fear that it will die. For instance, television, with its advertising, talk shows, and football games, is a huge teaching machine, teaching competitive values that no amount of formal schooling is going to eradicate. The value of de-emphasizing competition in school is to redress the balance somewhat.)

Besides these reasons for abolishing grades, the whole system of grades supports an erroneous conception of growth and the learning processes. Natural growth does not take place on a constant upward incline, but rather by fits and starts, with regressions and plateaus. Indiscriminate grading that catches one student during a spurt and another at a regression point leaves the impression that one is smarter than the other, has learned more, worked harder, etc. The student who is tested at a regression point may be so demoralized that his entire academic career and perhaps his whole life is affected.

I suspect that one of the major causes of dyslexia (inability to read) is the self-denigration that occurs when a child who is not emotionally or developmentally ready to synthesize the various processes that make up reading is given signals that he is less-than-adequate in this skill. These signals can come as messages from the teacher ("You can do better than that.") or the parents ("How was reading today?") or by a grade (Reading—Unsat.). Reading is just one of the areas where a low grade can confirm a young person's fears that he is just not quite as good as other people, and the low grade may then be the trigger of an internal ineffectiveness spiral: The low grade leads to a low self-evaluation of the individual's own abilities which leads to low effort on his part, which leads to low achievement which leads to another low grade, which confirms the low self-evaluation and which continues the spiral downward to lower and lower stages.

The fact that administrators, teachers, parents, and students have come to accept grades, to rely on grades, to want grades, and in fact to feel that they need grades does not make it any more permissible to continue this invidious practice. It is almost a case of the prisoners who have come to rely on their chains and thus fear freedom. Grades have no socially redeeming value: Grades are not a useful motivator, they are not a useful evaluator, they are not a useful predictor, they are not a useful separator. Grades must be abolished.

Evaluation, on the other hand, must *not* be abolished. Evaluation is an important and useful activity in living and learning. Evaluation is the valuing process of placing values on past events by means of analysis and diagnosis and of placing values on future events in setting goals. Because it is based on value judgments, evaluation is a basically human rather than mechanical activity. So the fundamental questions for evaluators are first, "What do we want?" and then, "How can we judge whether or not we are getting what we want?"

The problem comes when we start focusing on the second question first, that is, when we first ask ourselves, what are the instruments that we can use for measuring? Take this example: Suppose you want to find out whether Johnny has a fever or not. The obvious evaluative instrument is the fever thermometer. But if this hasn't been invented yet, what can you do? You can look at his cheeks to see if they are flushed, feel his forehead, ask him, "Johnny, how do you feel?" Most likely you will not weigh him, although you have a very good set of scales, or measure his height with your fine ruler or listen to his heart with your excellent stethoscope. You probably will not use the thermometer on the side of the house either, because you know that it cannot measure such a fine distinction.

And yet in educational evaluation we are constantly using inappropriate and inaccurate instruments to make diagnoses and measure educational outcomes. This is what Abraham Maslow called "means-centering" as opposed to "problem-centering"; that is, we try to make our evaluations fit the means that we have rather than starting with the problem and then finding or constructing appropriate means to evaluate that problem.

Furthermore, most of our reliable evaluative instruments are designed to measure short-term learning while completely ignoring the long-term effects of a given practice. For instance, we measure young people for their skill and understanding in reading but seldom evaluate whether the means that we use to teach reading will lead our students to enjoy reading and to consider reading a useful part of their lives or whether in fact the means that we use to teach reading also teach our young people to hate reading so that they will never voluntarily pick up a book in their lives. How many people dread having to write a letter because of the way they were taught composition, or hate the thought of balancing their check book because of their early experience in learning addition? Even though we talk about schooling as preparation for life, these are some of the educational outcomes that we are less likely to evaluate.

Here is a brainstorming program which I have used as a quick avenue to evaluate learning experiences:

1. Brainstorm the ways in which you want people to be different after the experience than they were before (5 minutes).

2. Select no more than three or combine items on your list to make no more than three of the above.

3. Brainstorm behaviors that you would be willing to accept as evidence that the experience was successful—that is, that people are really different as you have determined in No. 2 (5 minutes).

4. Brainstorm behaviors that you could regard as evidence that the experience was not successful—that is, that people have not changed as you determined in No. 2 (5 minutes).

5. Brainstorm ways that you might go about collecting the evidence that you have listed in items three and four (5 minutes).

6. Brainstorm ways that you might display your evidence so that it is meaningful to someone else (5 minutes).

7. Go back over the material in the previous items and design an evaluation program which you will be able to carry out.

This program can be used for very narrow goals *(I want people to be different by being able to recite the nines table, which they could not do before)*, or the program can be used for larger goals *(I want people to be different by being able to make more rational decisions about their lives than they could before)*. Step five can include the use of standardized tests *(I will collect evidence that the students have learned multiplication by their performance on the Stanford Achievement test)*, or it can use subjective or unobtrusive measures *(I will collect evidence that students have improved their use of empathetic understanding by counting the frequency of put-down statements per hour of class time; a reduction in frequency will indicate an increase in empathy)*.

Most educational evaluation reminds me of the boy who lost a dime in a dark alley. He spent his time searching for it under the street light because there was more light there, but he never found his dime. The significant goals of education are hard to pin down, difficult to evaluate. The important thing is not to surrender—not to shift the focus to the things that are easy to do.

XIII:
DISCIPLINE AND BEHAVIOR CONTROL

Discipline in the classroom is such an individual affair, so colored by the specific mix of personalities and needs, that it is almost impossible to say anything that will seem satisfactory and realistic to an individual teacher with a specific behavior problem to cope with. There are, however, some rules that may help some individuals with some specific problems.

1. *Avoid ultimatums:* "If I catch you throwing one more spit ball, I'll . . . ." This is almost like throwing down a gauntlet. It marks the beginning of a duel of wits in which the student can hardly lose, the teacher hardly win. The ultimatum pins down the teacher to watching especially for the given behavior, judging whether or not it really occurred ("I was just throwing it in the wastebasket so I wouldn't be tempted again."), and then facing up to fulfilling the terms of his threat, whether he wants to or not. Ultimatums almost invariably backfire, and they seldom eliminate the unwanted activity.

2. *Avoid sarcasm:* "Can't you make more noise than that?" Students don't know how to handle sarcasm—is the teacher being nice or nasty—what does he really mean? Sarcasm makes most students feel put down and leaves them with a feeling that they need to get back somehow.

3. *When in doubt, delay.* Avoid hasty action. "I'm

really not sure just what to do about that. I'm going to think it over. In the meantime, let's go on with . . . ."

4. *Try to avoid contaminating the entire life of the student.* Keep school problems at school, no matter how great the temptation is to turn the parents loose on the offender. Warnings sent home have such varied and unforeseen consequences that they are almost sure to leave a residue of resentment, which the student will sooner or later express.

5. *Look for realistic steps toward compliance.* "Sit with your hands folded in silence for the rest of the period," may seem like a good idea at the time, but "Let me have your unbroken attention for the next two minutes —Johnny, here's the stop watch, you keep time," is more likely to work.

6. Remember that behavior is generally motivated as a means of coping with some force or forces. *Try to understand the forces underlying acting-out behavior.* (Need for security? Attention? Self-respect? Love? Revenge?)

7. *Use the behavior problem as a learning experience wherever possible.* The problem almost inevitably is the result of a conflict of wills. Try to identify what is being willed by whom, and then work for a no-lose resolution where all parties can come away with the feeling that their rights have been respected and they have not lost self-esteem. Perhaps the most important thing that the teacher can teach is how to work on changing a conflict situation to one where each party understands the other and respects the other so that they can work on resolving the problem rather than besting the other person.

8. *Try to avoid thinking of the student as a problem.* He may cause problems for you, but he is not *per se* a problem. If you think of a student as a problem,

he is not likely to disappoint you. Teachers often un-
consciously narrow the range of acceptable behaviors
for problem students—they watch them more closely
and find more faults as a result. It's a self-fulfilling
prophecy.

9. *Take ownership of the problem.* If Billy knocks
his books on the floor and disturbs your instructions,
the problem is yours, not his: You are the one that
wants quiet so that you can be understood. (This does
not imply that you are the *cause* of the unwanted behavior, only that you are the one to whom the behavior
is a problem). This changes your manner of addressing
Billy from "Why can't you act your age?" or "What's
the matter with you now?" to "I'm sorry, Billy, my
problem is that I need you to be quiet while I'm giving
directions," or "I need your help—no one will understand me if you make too much noise."

10. *Take ownership of your own feelings.* If you are
irritated and upset, say so. "I'm sorry, I feel irritated
and upset because of your actions, and I'm finding it
very hard to think what is the fair thing for me to do."

11. *Avoid physical and psychological force wherever possible.* Both kinds of force drive the symptoms
of basic needs underground. In an extreme case you
may have a quieter class but slashed tires. And the use
of force teaches the use of force. Where parents and
teachers use force to get their way, children learn that
you can get your way if you're big enough and tough
enough.

XIV:
THE CLASSROOM AS LIVING ROOM:
NOTES ON THE USE OF SPACE

To paraphrase Dr. Harold Gores, Director of the Ford Foundation's Educational Facilities Laboratory, education is a fluid process which pretty much conforms to the space assigned to it. Where our classrooms are shoe boxes lined up neatly along a double-loaded corridor, we tend to think in shoe-box terms, putting English in this shoe box, history in that, math in the next; or fifth grade in this shoe box, fourth grade in the box across the hall. On the other hand, where the classroom area is a vast open space with no guides or clues as to what things are likely to go on in what part of the desert, then people find it difficult to figure out what they are doing there and how they can find their way. To accommodate human beings who are actively engaged in growing and changing, classrooms need definition and diversity—comfortable, well-lighted places for reading; dark, intimate places for being alone and thinking; informal sitting areas for group discussions; places to be loud and places to be quiet; visually interesting places—in short, rooms for living, living rooms.

There's not much that most teachers can do about the bricks and concrete and plaster that make up their classrooms. Some are limited as to the things that they can put on their walls. Many would risk being fired by just suggesting that the school buy an old arm chair, a sofa, or a couple of hassocks to put in their classroom. And the janitor would most likely complain if a teacher brought in an old rug to cover a section of the gray asphalt tile floor.

And yet in some schools some of these things are possible. In some situations teachers can change the climate of their classrooms by introducing an odd piece of livingroom furniture or two, by partitioning off a small section of the room with movable bookshelves for a thinking corner, or by setting up a reading area with a couple of old mattresses covered with bright bedspreads and pillows and with a bridge lamp or two for special illumination. Other teachers have been able to keep three or four throw rugs which can be spread out for sitting on to play games, talk, or read, and then be rolled up and stored on the shelf. A bunch of pillows can be used in the same way.

Teachers who are unable to do any of the above may at least be able to alter the traditional seating pattern so that the students can sit in a circle, a horseshoe, clusters, or some other informal arrangement. And most teachers can introduce some aspects of visual stimulation by bringing collages, mobiles, posters, and other kinds of art and sculpture into the classroom. (Many art museums have special collections to loan to classroom teachers). Teachers who move from room to room report that it is well worth the time to rearrange the furniture at the beginning and end of the period, and I know one travelling teacher who takes her own folding display board from class to class.

Making the classroom an attractive and comfortable place for human beings—a living room—is neither just a nice frill nor a physical manifestation of a permissive, do-your-own-thing and slouch-where-you-please philosophy. The classroom-living room sends messages to the people in the room—messages of safety, security, belongingness, and warmth: messages which say that this is a place where the individual is respected and trusted, where human beings may engage in human activity.

Making the classroom into a living room helps to fill our basic needs, ease our anxieties, and promote our learning. As a living room, the classroom can begin to promote a new interest in and awareness of learning. For here learning no longer must be seen as some strange, arcane experience that goes on only where five rows of six small, hard student desks confront the big teacher's desk and the blackboard at the focus of the room: Here learning can be seen as living.

XV:
NOTES ON CREATIVE THINKING

Schools as they exist today seem to be set up specifically for the purpose of squashing creative thinking. Grades, tests, textbooks, teacher-as-evaluator, a one-right-answer, one-right-way atmosphere, formica-topped desks, standard curriculum units, the forty-minute period, all insure that individual creative thinking will be devalued and destroyed.

I'm not talking here about art and music and poetry and dance and the like. These "creative" arts are already devalued by their minor place in the curriculum. (*Frills* is the general term applied to them in budget meetings.) Art is Tuesday and Thursday from two until three, unless somebody more important like the Public Health officer shows up. Music is learning the songs that the music teacher likes; poetry is never graded; dance is only for girls. Art and music and poetry and dance *could* be powerful forces in developing creative thinking, but in most instances they have been emasculated in today's schools.

I'm thinking, instead, of creative thinking as applicable to any subject, any area of life. Science, math, history, literature, all are built on the discoveries of creative thinkers. When we examine some of the great creative thinkers—Darwin, Galileo, Beethoven, we discover that their creations were, in reality, making something new out of something old: not creating little pieces and then placing them together so much as seeing the little pieces that were already lying around and fitting them together in a new way. Creative thinking is finding the keystone to complete the arch, or turning the world upside down and standing at the edge, rather than at the center, of the universe. If education is seen as the transmission of old knowledge into new heads, then creative thinking has no place. But if education is the systematic encouragement of the human potential to find new ways of living—of surviving, then creative thinking is central to the school.

Creative thinking dies in an authoritarian atmosphere, thrives in an atmosphere of psychological freedom and security. When I feel free to speculate, to toy with ideas, to think outrageous and bizarre thoughts, without the threat of loss of self-esteem or the withdrawal of respect, love, friendship, or protection, then I am free to create. When I feel outside forces attempting to control, coerce, limit, or evaluate my thinking, then I feel threatened, and my creative energy is syphoned off into responding to the threat.

Carl Rogers has identified three psychological conditions which foster creativity.[1] First is *openness to experience*. This means being continually aware of new perceptions as they come in. Instead of seeing things in predetermined categories ("Grass is green." "Going to church is good," "Manure smells bad."), the individual can be aware of his own perceptions at the moment and without regard to the usual categories ("*This* grass is purple." "Going to church *this time* is harmful." "*This* manure has a rather pleasant odor"). The individual who is open to experience resists the temptation to establish rigid categories; he tolerates and even

---

[1] Carl Rogers, "Towards a Theory of Creativity," in Sidney J. Parnes and Harold F. Harding (eds.), *A Source Book for Creative Thinking* (New York: Charles Scribner's Sons, 1962).

delights in ambiguity, and he is able to receive and hold conflicting information without forcing premature closure on a situation. The individual who is open to experience realizes that reality is not a series of easily defined givens, but rather a flow of events which are unique, vague, amorphous, and ambiguous.

The second condition for the fostering of creativity is *an internal locus of evaluation.* This is perhaps the most fundamental condition for fostering creativity. For the creative individual, the value of his product is not determined by the praise or criticism of outside agents, but by himself: My product is satisfying to *me.* It fills my basic needs for self-respect, for self-expression, for joy. If I am forced to consider the probable praise or criticism of others at each step along the way, then part of my vital energy is diverted from my creation into attempts to evaluate what it is that others would wish for. And my creative power is lessened as a result.

This is not to say that the creative person should be oblivious to the judgments of others or of their reactions to him and his product. This feedback is an important part of shaping the person's concepts of himself and of his society. It does mean, though, that the basis of evaluation lies within himself in his own organismic reaction to his own product. The product is satisfying to his basic urge to create.

The third condition is *the ability to play,* to toy with the world. This implies an ability to live solely for the moment without regard for future consequences. Living for the moment enhances the ability to be open to new experience, to go off on a wild goose chase, to catch and ride a hunch. Playing also implies the ability to toss and juggle, to shape elements and ideas into wild juxtapositions and improbable hypotheses. This spontaneous toying gives rise to new combinations and surprises. It allows for the possibility of seeing life in new and significant ways. It is from this rich jumble of chaos that the new spark of creativity often jumps.

How can we imbue the classroom with these conditions that foster creativity? What can we do to allow for spontaneous play and internal evaluation? How can we build delight in the ambiguous, the different, and the unknown? I doubt that the answer lies in merely letting everyone do his own thing. The answer belongs with the teacher. Where the teacher takes delight in novelty, in ambiguity, in absurdity; where the teacher fosters an atmosphere of joy and play and helps supply the materials, words, colors, music, costumes; where the teacher steadfastly refuses to evaluate the creative output of the student and helps the student to be strong enough to rely on his own internal evaluation—there will be the classroom which encourages creativity.

XVI:
NOTES ON ROLE-TAKING AS A MEANS OF DEVELOPING MORAL JUDGMENT

The principal traditional conception of teaching for moral development has been to drill in a set of fixed moral virtues, such as honesty, helpfulness, willingness to obey, etc. The teacher displays the virtue by precept and example and moral tales and then rewards the students for conforming to the virtue and punishes them for failure to conform. It is a teaching method which has been noticeably unsuccessful.

Recently, however, a newer conception of moral judgment training has begun to emerge. Starting with John Dewey and then Piaget, and most recently refined by Lawrence Kohlberg, this conception starts with the assumption that the formation of moral judgment is a process of development through stages of knowing —that is, a process of growing awareness of the external world.

If we agree with Dewey, Piaget, and Kohlberg that the development of moral judgment is a cognitive, a knowing process, rather than the absorption of an imposed set of standards, then rather than lecture and preach to our students about the importance of honesty, responsibility, helpfulness, etc., it is clearly the job of teachers to set up learning experiences which will facilitate moral development.

These experiences fall under the general category of what Kohlberg calls role-taking: that is, opportunities to take a variety of socially useful roles so that the individual will be able to see a moral decision from a number of different perspectives. The wider the range of role-experience of the individual, the more likely he is to make a moral decision that will be just and satisfactory to many rather than to his single perspective. The operating factor in role-taking is empathy. The more an individual is able to empathize with others, the more likely he is to make a just moral decision.

How then can we create learning opportunities that foster role-taking, that develop the power of empathy? By setting up situations where students can engage in a variety of socially useful tasks, where students can be given both responsibility and a share in decision-making at appropriate levels, where students can see their own importance to the society in which they live.

Some classrooms are naturally better adapted to provide role-taking opportunities than others. The classroom where students serve as student and teacher, as cook, cookie server, blackboard washer, builder of airplanes, and planner of activities is more likely to promote role-taking than the classroom where students are encouraged to act only as students, respond only to the teacher, and are forced to await their turn for a drink of water sitting quietly with their hands folded until the person in front of them has returned from the drinking fountain.

Role-playing is another way to promote empathy. Role-playing is a sort of simulated role-taking. When young children dress up as "mother" and "father" and engage in fanciful play, they are beginning to play the role of another person, beginning to build their power of empathy. The elementary school classroom which has a costume box and plenty of opportunities for children to engage in this informal role-playing is naturally encouraging moral development.

For older students, role-playing social problems is an important way of gaining empathetic insight into another person's perspective on life. Students can be asked to role-play the new boy in class, the highway builder and the farmer, Lieutenant Calley at My Lai, and a long list of real and hypothetical roles in which moral decisions must be made. Through placing themselves in a role and experiencing the processes of deciding, students can begin to see moral deciding in a larger framework than their single point-of-view.

Ultimately all formal education should be moral education. The school should be a place where each individual's activity can also be social in character—where the student by working in and on his physical environment can develop as an individual and at the same time use his powers to further the larger activities of the group. That is, he should be given the opportunities to play many socially useful roles. It is the moral responsibility of the teacher to supply every possible aid to this process.

XVII:
NOTES ON THE
AUTHORITARIAN PERSONALITY

Much of formal education seems designed specifically to develop an authoritarian personality in students.
The norms of passivity and submission to authority,
the emphasis on conformity and one right answer, the
value placed on neatness over creativity and uniformity
over individuality, the arbitrary exercise of power ev-
ident in the setting up of the curriculum and in determining how and what to grade, and even the loud-
speaker system which clearly indicates a hierarchy of
authority with the principal at the top and the student at
the bottom, all leave their stamp, all teach the values of
authority and certainty.

The problem is that these values are not congruent
with the real world, where no authority lasts for long
and the only certainties are death and taxes.

For the individual, authoritarianism diminishes the
ability to adapt to a changing world; for society, authoritarianism diminishes our chance to survive. The
authoritarian individual who is unable to accept new
ways of doing things, who is unable to adjust his life to
the new realities, lives out his days in bitterness and
frustration. The society that brings old answers—like
the waging of war, the filling in of swamps and marsh-
es, the raising of tariffs, to new problems—like the population explosion, the limitations of natural resources,

the new international economy, that society is destined for destruction.

In this sense authoritarianism can be seen as a personality disorder, rather common in nature, but nonetheless serious in consequence. When a nation's schools foster authoritarian personality development, this decreases the creative talent available to solve emerging problems and increases the likelihood that old and unrealistic solutions will be tried. The prime example of this self-destructiveness of authoritarianism is, of course, Hitler's Germany.

The answer to authoritarian training is not, however, *laissez-faire*, everybody do his own thing. *Laissez-faire* education often leads to dissipation, disorganization, frustration, and a gradual drift back towards authoritarianism as an answer. (Summerhill is a good example of this: generally *laissez-faire* with an occasional lapse into authoritarianism to pull things together.) The alternative to authoritarian training is an education which will help the individual find the means to fill his basic needs and which will support him as he moves toward social-self-actualization.

XVIII:
MEANS VALUES, END VALUES,
AND SOCIAL ENTROPY

Entropy is the natural tendency of systems to break down, lose their special purposes, become undifferentiated, and fall into sameness and chaos. For example, I developed a system of putting special and important telephone numbers on the outside back cover of the phone book. First to be listed was the pizza parlor so that I could quickly order up my Monday night special. Then came my doctor's number. My wife added the numbers of two babysitters. An emergency showed the importance of including the plumber's number there. And then a friend who had recently moved called from Oshkosh, and I added his number along with a few doodles. And so on. You can see, of course, what's happening. Now, today, the back cover is practically useless. And I've begun a new system: When I find one of my important numbers, like the pizza parlor, I circle it in red so that I will be able to find it easily.

The curriculum is very much like that. As more and more important things are identified for inclusion, it gets harder and harder to sort out what is important. Because we have reached the point of teaching everything all the time, we are in reality teaching nothing but a big, confusing blur. Of course, reading is very important, and so we teach it. And so is algebra, and so composition, and the semi-colon (very important that); and Shakespeare and the Civil War; and now Sex Education and Drug Abuse Education, to the point that it's all just another thing to take, so far as the student is concerned.

What we need is a clear notion of the difference between means values and end values. For instance, I value writing as a means of communicating with others. I value church as a means of religious expression, fire as a means of cooking my food, warming my family, and stimulating my reverie (as in front of an open fireplace). For me writing, church, and fire are means values. If other and better ways are found to accomplish the ends that they serve, then I can do without them. When they no longer serve me, then I should, in fact must, do without them.

The problem with means values is that as they serve us, they dress themselves in the clothes of end values, becoming ends in themselves. Thus the familiar "Go to church this Sunday" type of public service advertising, extolling the virtues of church-going rather than of religious expression. "Support the College of Your Choice" and "Stay in School" campaigns are of similar nature—an unconscious shifting of means values (What is college for? What is a high school diploma for?) so that they become ends in themselves despite the fact that they may no longer serve a beneficial social function. (Recent research indicates, for instance, that staying in high school may do more harm for some young people than dropping out).

When we identify a means value, the proper question to ask is *what end does this serve?* In the case of church (means value) the end served is religious expression, and church attendance may be a useful means to attain this end. But when church is seen as the only means to religious expression, or when church-going is seen as an absolute good in its own right, then entropic drift has occurred and society winds up serving a value that was instituted to serve society. Another example is the study of Latin. Latin is useful in developing English vocabulary (means value). But if the development of a good vocabulary is an end value, then we should take a look at the other possible means of developing vocabulary—studying word lists, extensive reading, conversation, watching television, etc. When we say that Latin is useful for developing vocabulary and therefore eveyone should study Latin, a clear entropic drift has occurred. Literature is a means of exploring and understanding the human condition. It may even be the best means. Certainly "the classics" have much to offer in the way of vicarious experience. But when this is translated into an end value, such as everyone should read *Hamlet* or *War and Peace*, then we must waste our precious energy forcing *Hamlet* or *War and Peace* on an unwilling population under the notion that this and only this is *good for them.*

Social entropy occurs when the means values which are created to maintain and improve the social order become non-productive, false end values in themselves and require social energy for their maintenance, a sort of social equivalent to drug addiction. The drug which once served as a means to joy and pleasure now requires that maintenance, support, and physical energy be given to it.

An understanding of social entropy is important to education for two reasons: First, entropy thrives in the schoolhouse. It is the one peril of the ivory tower: Latin teachers an orderly mind, algebra teaches logic, it is the essential mark of an educated person that he be fluent in at least one European language (that means French, of course, or possibly German), team sports teach the importance of teamwork and interdependence, and so on and so on. The people responsible for setting up and maintaining educational programs need to ask them-

Plate III
MEANS VALUES, END VALUES, AND THE
ENTROPIC DRIFT TOWARD FALSE END VALUES

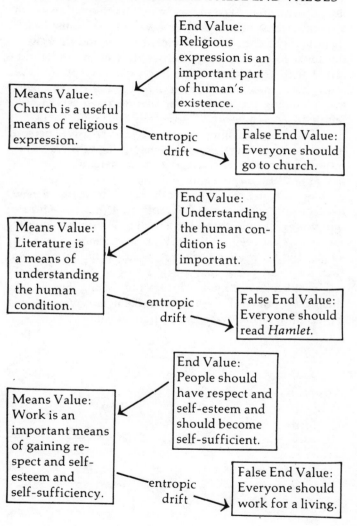

selves again and again, "How does this serve us, how does this serve society?" We must test each value, each piece of curriculum, each institution against this notion of entropy. Second, we must train our young to discern means values and end values; we must teach them to fight entropy. This means equipping them with the tools to see the new realities in a changing world, rather than relying on older, less valid perceptions. We must train them to see their lives and their world as ever-changing processes rather than as fixed sets of certainties.

The distinguishing mark of the creative person is that he can see old problems in new ways. This means accepting, encouraging, and delighting in the new, the different, the unusual—not merely because it is new or unusual, but because it may throw some new light on our most complex problems. We must educate our young people to this creativity. We must educate them to resist seeing the world as a series of givens, of single right answers, of pre-ordained limitations, so that they can bring new insight to our intractable social problems. We must educate our young people for their own survival by teaching them survival skills—by teaching them how to live by human values.

Appendix A:
SUGGESTIONS FOR FURTHER READING

Assagioli, Roberto, M.D. *Psychosynthesis*. New York: Viking Press, 1965. A presentation of the theory and practice of a major school of existential psychotherapy with an emphasis on the development of the will. Many implications and some specific applications for educators.

Bach, Richard. *Jonathan Livingston Seagull*. New York: Macmillan Company, 1970. You too can fly!

Brown, George Isaac. *Human Teaching for Human Learning*. New York: Viking Press, 1971. An introduction to confluent education, that is, the combining of affective and cognitive learning. Gestalt oriented. Many useful activities are described in passing.

Glasser, William, M.D. *Schools Without Failure*. New York: Harper & Row, 1969. Presents sound rationale to abolish grading plus some useful alternatives. Also an exposition of Glasser's "classroom meeting" technique.

Gordon, W. J. J. *The Metaphorical Way of Learning and Knowing*. Cambridge, Mass.: Porpoise Books, 1971. Synectics applied to the classroom. An exciting approach to unlocking the doors of creativity in students.

Greer, Mary, and Bonnie Rubinstein. *Will the Real Teacher Please Stand Up: A Primer in Humanistic Education*. Pacific Palisades, Calif.: Goodyear Publishing Co., 1972. Many activities and some useful theory.

Hawley, Robert C. and Isabel L. Hawley. *A Handbook of Personal Growth Activities for Classroom Use*. Amherst, Mass.: Education Research Associates, 1972. Ninety-four activities to promote personal and social growth with rationale for each. Naturally I think that this is a super book.

Holt, John. *How Children Fail.* New York: Dell Publishing Co., 1964. An awareness-raising book. Required reading for all parents and teachers.

_____.*What Do I Do Monday?* New York: Dell, 1970. Many useful ideas for classroom teachers.

Jones, Muriel, and Dorothy Jorgenward. *Born to Win.* Reading, Mass.: Addison-Wesley, 1971. A combination of Gestalt Therapy and Transactional Analysis as an aid to understanding behavior and promoting growth. Includes specific techniques for teachers.

Kirschenbaum, Howard, Sidney Simon, and Rodney Napier. *Wad-Ja-Get? The Grading Game in American Education.* New York: Hart Publishing Co., 1971. A novel approach to exposition of the damaging effects of the grading system and what one fictional high school did about it. Excellent annotated bibliography of research on grading.

Maslow, Abraham H. *Motivation and Personality,* 2nd ed. New York: Harper & Row, 1970. Every teacher should be forced to memorize this book. One of the cornerstones in humanistic psychological theory.

Overly, Norman V. (ed.). *The Unstudied Curriculum: Its Impact on Children.* Washington, D.C.: Association for Supervision and Curriculum Development, 1970. Many thought-provoking essays including a concise statement by Lawrence Kohlberg of his theory and research in the development of moral judgment.

Perls, Frederick S., M.D., Ph. D. *Gestalt Therapy Verbatim.* Lafayette, Calif.: Real People Press, 1969. Transcripts of tapes by Fritz Perls, the founder of Gestalt Therapy. The most useful statement of what Gestalt is all about that I have come across.

Postman, Neil, and Charles Weingartner. *Teaching as a Subversive Activity*. New York: Dell Publishing Co., 1969. Argues that education should be a process of challenging the assumptions of society in order to test their validity. Many examples of how teachers can change their classroom behaviors to promote social a-wareness in their students.

Prince, George M. *The Practice of Creativity: A Manual for Dynamic Group Problem Solving*. New York: Harper & Row, 1970. An exposition of the "Synectic" problem-solving technique—ways to enhance creative problem-solving.

Raths, Louis E., Merrill Harmin, & Sidney B. Simon. *Values and Teaching: Working with Values in the Classroom*. Columbus, Ohio: Charles E. Merrill, 1966. This is the original values clarification manual. It contains the rationale and a wealth of useful value-clarifying activities.

Rogers, Carl. *Freedom to Learn*. Columbus, Ohio: Charles E. Merrill, 1969. Rogers' manifesto on education. One of the foundations of humanistic education.

Schmuck, Richard A. and Patricia A. Schmuck. *Group Processes in the Classroom*. Dubuque, Iowa: Wm. C. Brown Co., 1971. Recent research and some practical activities to help teachers become more effective facilitators of group processes.

Schrank, Jeffrey. *Teaching Human Beings: 101 Subversive Activities for the Classroom*. Boston: Beacon Press, 1972. Chapters on teaching about drugs, death, and violence, among others. Many references to ways to integrate film and other media into the classroom, with listings of films and other source materials.

Shaftel, Fannie R. and George Shaftel. *Role-Playing for Social Values: Decision-Making in the Social Studies*. Englewood Cliffs, N.J.: Prentice-Hall, 1967.

The book on role-playing. Especially useful for social studies teachers in grades five through eight.

Simon, Sidney B., Robert C. Hawley, and David D. Britton. *Composition for Personal Growth: Values Clarification Through Writing.* New York: Hart Publishing Co., 1973. Originally designed for English teachers but easily adaptable by any teacher trying to humanize his or her classroom, this book contains a myriad of useful and practical ideas for classroom teachers.

Simon, Sidney, Leland Howe, and Howard Kirschenbaum. *Values Clarification: A Handbook of Practical Strategies.* New York: Hart Publishing Co., 1972. Chock full of useful value-clarifying techniques.

Spolin, Viola. *Improvisation for the Theater: A Handbook of Teaching and Directing Techniques.* Evanston, Ill.: Northwestern University Press, 1963. *The* book on improvisational theatre: Full of useful teaching games and insights about how students learn.

Weinstein, Gerald, and Mario D. Fantini (eds.). *Toward Humanistic Education: A Curriculum of Affect.* New York: Praeger, 1970. A rationale for affective curriculum with several useful activities. Presents the "Trumpet," a model for integrating concerns, thought, and action.

Appendix B:

E R A TEACHER
COMMUNICATION INVENTORY

How do my students see me? Try to think how your students might rate you on each of these continuums. What behaviors of yours do you expect raise defensiveness in students? What behaviors do you expect raise supportiveness? .

DEFENSE-RAISING   SUPPORTIVE

Evaluative---------1---2---3---4---5---6---7--- Descriptive
(Sending value-laden   (Sending descriptive
messages).   messages).

Controlling--------1---2---3---4---5---6---7--- Cooperative
(Sending messages that   (Sending messages that
say, "I want to control   say, "I want to work
you").   with you").

Hidden ------------1---2---3---4---5---6---7--- Open
(Sending messages which   (Sending messages which
seem to have a hidden   are open, direct, and
purpose).   clear).

Neutral-----------1---2---3---4---5---6---7--- Empathetic
(Sending messages that   (Sending messages that
show a lack of concern for   show concern for the
the feelings, attitudes   feelings, attitudes, and
and beliefs of the students). beliefs of students).

Superior----------1---2---3---4---5---6---7--- Equal
(Sending messages which   (Sending messages that
identify the teacher as   play down the superiority
superior in power, know-   of the teacher).
ledge, authority, etc.).

Certain-----------1---2---3---4---5---6---7--- Provisional
(Sending messages which indicate   (Sending messages which
that the teacher is certain,   indicate that the teacher
sure, and not open to modifi-   considers his information
cation of his ideas).   as provisional, subject to
                                    change on the basis of
                                    additional data).

To improve your communication patterns in the classroom pick one or two items where your students might rate your behavior as defense-raising. Then brainstorm ways to modify your behavior so that your communication will engender more support in that area. Pick one idea and self-contract to practice the new behavior.

Appendix C:
AN APPROACH TO INTER-DISCIPLINARY TEACHING

I. Use the sequence of teaching concerns: Orientation; Community-Building; Achievement Motivation; Fostering Open Communication; Information Seeking, Gathering, and Sharing; Value Exploration and Clarification; Planning for Change.

II. Identify and explore student concerns using personal growth activities and relevant material from the academic disciplines most immediately concerned.

III. Build inter-disciplinary learning opportunities based on key concepts. These are concepts which adults judge to be important for young people to understand but which young people may be unaware of because of a lack of experience (e.g. prejudice, the nines table, power and powerlessness, the human circulatory system, international balance of payments, body language, the decimal system, the relationship of the individual to society).

The following procedure can be used:

A. Identify those key concepts which are important for students' awareness and growth but which students do not recognize because of lack of experience.

B. Select a concept and determine duration of unit. (The breadth or narrowness of definition of the concept must correlate with the amount of time available for its exploration).

C. Establish goals (to be augmented or modified later by in-put from students).

D. Set up situations where students will encounter the concept experientially (either through actual encounter or through simulation).

E. Explore these experiences through discussion and value-clarifying activities.

F. Introduce relevant materials from the disciplines.

For example:

A. Prejudice, racial discrimination, the position of ethnic minorities in American society, powerlessness, . . .

B. Racial discrimination: three weeks (5 class periods per week).

C. To make white, middle class, suburban students aware of what it feels like to be always an underdog with no escape.

D. Simulation—brown-eyed students get special privileges, blue-eyed students get special handicaps.

E. Discuss feelings and ask for values cards on the experience.

F. *Black Like Me, Manchild in the Promised Land, Raisin in the Sun, The Merchant of Venice,* descriptions of slave auctions, unemployment statistics broken down by ethnic groups (past as well as present), etc., etc., etc.

Appendix D:
GENERIC PERSONAL GROWTH ACTIVITIES

Any activity which heightens self- and social-awareness or promotes creativity is a personal growth activity. The following is a listing of generic activities which have been found useful in many settings.

Forced-choice problems

Rank-order

Continuums

Sentence stems

Inventories and pattern searches

Role-plays and simulations

Sense awareness activities

Fantasy trips

Questionnaires, value sheets, feedback forms

Brainstorming

Metaphor and personal analogy

Art, dance, music

Theater games

Sensitizing modules

Directed reflection, written or non-written

Voting and polling

Additions:

Appendix E:
A CONVERSATION AMONG TEACHERS

Note: In January 1973 Edgar C. Alward and Robert C. Hawley conducted an intensive course entitled "Communication for Personal and Social Growth" at the Western Massachusetts Regional Office of the State Department of Education in Springfield under the sponsorship of Westfield State College. The following is excerpted from a follow-up conference held at the beginning of February.

GEORGE (social studies teacher, middle school): I've been doing a unit called "Parents and Children" with one of my seventh grade groups. We're trying to get at whether or not there really is a generation gap, and if so, what to do about it. I guess that the first part is sort of a consciousness-raising business. I showed the film "Claude."[1] It's only three minutes, and in it there's a boy building something in a little black box while his parents are around paying him no attention. Then he throws the switch and they disappear. That's the end of the film. The kids were really interested, and we discussed what had happened, and especially what the boy had done to his parents.

BOB: What did they think?

GEORGE: Well, it was funny. Nobody thought that the boy had killed his parents. They really couldn't explain.

ED: I wonder if any of the students wished they had their own little black boxes.

GEORGE: Well, I asked them that, and most would like to have one just for certain times. Mostly when their

---

[1] "Claude" produced by Dan McLaughlin, distributed by Pyramid Films, Santa Monica, California.

parents yell at them or else won't listen. Those seem to be the two things that really bother the kids.

BOB: Maybe because yelling and not listening are two signs that the kids take to mean that their parents don't value them as human beings. It means a loss of self-respect.

MARY (fifth grade teacher): But aren't there some times when a parent yells at a child because she loves him? I think I do.

BOB: That's right; but it's not the motives of the parent that count here; it's the perception of the child. Yelling apparently fails to communicate the love and respect that the parent may feel.

GEORGE: Then we used the "Marijuana Story" as a follow-up. It's in the *Handbook*.[2] If you're not familiar with it, it's a little story involving the generation gap. Then I asked the students to rank the five characters in order from the one whose actions they most approved to the one whose actions they least approved. The thing that really bothered them in the story was that the parents wouldn't listen to the youngsters.

ED: That's interesting. I think we find that that kind of not listening is characteristic of teacher behavior in the classroom, too.

GEORGE: Yes, and that reminds me of one more thing: Since I've been taking this course, I've been having my students move their desks into a circle instead of having rows. I'm what they call a "floating teacher," that is, I don't have a room of my own, and so I have to have them arrange the desks at the beginning of the period

---

[2]Robert C. Hawley and Isabel L. Hawley, *A Handbook of Personal Growth Activities for Classroom Use* (Amherst, Mass.: Education Research Associates, 1972).

and then put them back at the end because the other teachers don't like it that way.

BOB: I wish you could get the other teachers to try it.

GEORGE: The kids were funny the first time I tried it. They thought that the class was being rude because they started speaking directly to one another without waiting for me to lead the discussion. But now they really like it. In fact, one day last week I was late getting into a class, and they had already set up the desks in a circle.

BOB: One of the things that I'm hearing is that even though it takes five to ten minutes out of the period to arrange the desks, you feel it's worth it, that is, you get more done in that less time.

GEORGE: Oh, yes, Very definitely, There's one other thing: I've always enjoyed teaching, but I really look forward to my classes more now. Even though it takes me an extra half-hour a night to prepare.

BOB: That's something that really concerns me. One of the things that we have to keep working on is ways to do some of that planning during the school day so as to prevent teacher burn-out. I mean, you can keep up giving a half-hour or an hour extra to your school work just for so long. You've got to leave time for yourself, or you'll just wear out too fast.

ED: In many ways it's like being a beginning teacher all over again. It takes longer to prepare now, but once you get used to it, I think it will take less time. When I started using these methods, I nearly worked myself to death. But now I've sort of developed a rhythm, and some things come more naturally to me.

MARTY (seventh grade English teacher): Well, I did something that was very simple—it's in the *Handbook* on page thirty-nine—and that's *Letters to the Teacher*. I've been setting aside part of a period every other week for students to write me a private letter. Then I read them and write something back on each one and return them. It's been very successful. I've gotten to know my students a lot better. When I see them in the hall and say "Hi," I feel that there's more between us than before, that is, we have more things in common. This is one that I didn't let anybody "pass" on. I felt that everybody could have something to say to me. One girl said that it was stupid and then went on to write two pages of very personal and important things that she wanted to say to me.

RUTH (elementary learning disabilities specialist): It's too bad that you couldn't write a letter back to each one. They love to receive letters.

MARTY: I've got over a hundred students, so I really can't do that. But I do put a little note on each one.

BOB: That's very important. Something so that they know you've read and understood. Nothing kills that kind of program faster than having those letters disappear so that they don't know whether you've even looked at them or not. The other thing that kills *Letters to the Teacher* dead is if you comment on mechanics, spelling, handwriting, and so forth . . . .

It seems that what we come down to talking about again and again is open communication. What other ways are you using to open up communication in your classes?

MARY (fifth grade teacher): Well, I've noticed that since I've started sitting on the floor with my kids that they have been much more open. We have some great discussions now.

BOB: You and your children are on the same level. It seems that just the physical setting has a lot to do with open communication—being on the same level or all sitting in a circle and so on.

LEO (seventh and eighth grade English teacher): We've been doing something in the way of community-building that you might call opening communication: Last Monday we made a class telephone directory and then for their assignment everyone called everyone else. We've been telephoning like crazy. The first night I gave out an assignment over the phone, which was to bring a blindfold and an orange for the next day's class. Then in class we did an activity from the blue book[3] where everybody picks out his own orange blindfolded. They all got their own oranges back, and then, of course, they ate them. Then the next night I sent them home with sealed envelopes. The envelopes contained a copy of the "Marijuana Story" and somebody's phone number to call and try to convince each other about which of the characters did the best thing and so on. On the third night I asked everybody to watch the same TV program and then to call somebody and discuss it.

BOB: Oh, telephoning, that's a great idea! Did everybody get a call?

LEO: Yes, they worked it out in class so that everybody would get at least one call. And of course they could make as many as they wanted.

ED: Did you have any students who had no phone?

LEO: There were a couple, but they had some kind of access, and that worked out all right. One thing, if you're going to try it: Be sure to have a copy of the phone book because some of the kids can't remember their own numbers.

ED: Here is something that's a product of our technology that can be really useful in teaching. I bet that stu-

---

[3] *Composition for Personal Growth* by Sidney B. Simon, Robert C. Hawley, and David D. Britton—a special prepublication edition with blue cover put out by Education Research Associates, Amherst, Mass.

dents learn to listen better over the telephone, too. And yet the telephone is such an ordinary thing that you'd never really think of it for something like that.

BOB: You know, the things we've been talking about are not really very spectacular or elaborate, but I've a feeling that they make a real difference in the lives of our students, and in our own lives as well.

Participants:

> *Leo Alvares*
> *Ed Alward*
> *Marty Conroy*
> *George Elsner*

> *Bob Hawley*
> *Ruth Holman*
> *Mary Rix*

Appendix F:
LETTERS FROM TEACHERS

The following are excerpts from letters received by the author from teachers who have been using personal and social growth approaches in their classes. They are included here because they record specific changes in teacher behavior as the teachers work toward making the teaching of human values the central concern of their classrooms.

1.

I'm finding out how much I have been relying on old-time authoritarian muscle to keep these kids in line and how impossible that muscle is in this kind of a workshop[1] . . . . The best days with the program are those days when I am most relaxed and the kids aren't being bugged by too much me . . . . I'm also discovering how much I have been the central talker in the classroom and how little the kids know about how to proceed without me . . . . However the stuff is great and I'm enjoying what I'm learning about myself as well as what I see the kids learning.

—English teacher, high school

2.

In my teaching, I am being more overt and I'm more confident in justifying my methods to other teachers, since I am more sure that I am right in considering the child as a person, in any way I can.

Specifically, I have done pantomiming with my groups. In order to participate, each one writes his

---

[1] Reference is to the writing program set forth in *Composition for Personal Growth* by Sidney B. Simon, Robert C. Hawley, and David D. Britton (see Appendix A). This program has been used in a number of schools, principally in the New England area, since September 1971.

"act" in a sentence before he performs. Their sentences show a lot of thought this way. We've done some role playing, too. I found it helps to work out a familiar story at first. One group has a great time with "The Three Little Pigs." [We had] one hilarious session when I asked my group of boys to pretend Mother Pig decided to leave instead of sending them out. That really nudged their creativity.

One extremely inept language group made pictures of their favorite dinner, an outfit of clothes they would like to have, and how they would decorate their cave if they were cavemen. Then they wrote a sentence caption for each one. When they are interested, the quality of their work is remarkable . . . .

If we don't allow children to think original thoughts, we might as well quit. We can't supply the data for functioning in the future. We don't know what the future will be. Our duty is to allow a development of mental agility for coping with whatever the future presents.

—elementary level teacher of children with
special learning disabilities

3.

The activities I have used have met great response from my students! I feel good about arriving to school with colored paper and tinker toys and feel rewarded after class. *Composition for Personal Growth* has brought about some of my most memorable exciting moments in teaching! (Some of my students openly admit English is fun!)

—English teacher, high school

4.

There are many ways to make learning more interesting and relevant, and I am always on the lookout for them. . . . I have already tried the Blind Walk, building collages, from which we wrote haikus, constructing "love" with colored paper (no Tinker Toys available), and Either/Or [2] . . .

There are changes in my classroom. I am now making wider use of the circle. While we have always held many discussions on varied topics, never before have we sat on the floor with me right down in the middle. We almost always tape our discussions now; somehow, holding a mike seems to be conducive to speaking freely; ideas and opinions flow, and almost everyone is eager to contribute. Of course, the playback is the best of all, and the cassettes go into our interest corner for use and re-use. Also, we use the circle now for many formerly seat-oriented activities—social studies discussion and review, arithmetic fact drill, composition and report reading, poetry sessions, and just plain "let's talk" sessions. The response is tremendously exciting.

Another change is a freer exchange among groups. Always my children have worked in groups, but within their own groups; now they move from group to group or change groups whenever they feel that it would be helpful or even less dull. The room is now more mobile and more of a cooperative.

A third change is in the use of our interest center or classroom retreat. In one corner of the room is a screened-off area containing a library table, chairs (comfortable folding ones), books, research material, things to look at and feel (the children constantly renew exhibits), a cassette player and recorder with filled and blank tapes, a record player and records, and plenty of paper. The children love to use the center; they like the

---

[2] These activities are included in *A Handbook of Personal Growth Activities for Classroom Use* by Robert C. Hawley and Isabel L. Hawley (Amherst, Mass.: Education Research Associates, 1972).

feeling of apartness. Formerly they had to ask to use it when their work was done. Now they simply go there when they are free, and no one seems to abuse the privilege, for they recognize it as such. If the corner is full, they wait their turn, or someone relinquishes his place. Noise is kept at a minimum and never interferes with regular class work. It is the children's corner, and I never go there unless I am invited, that is when it is in use.

So you see, I have changed . . . . Whether I am a better teacher or not, I don't know, except that I know that I have grown, and growth is almost bound to make a better teacher. Well, we shall see. It is too soon to evaluate fully.

—fifth grade teacher

5.

I am so gratified by the closeness that has developed between my students and me since I began the thought-sharing ideas. We communicate on a totally different level, I understand them better and am aware of their *individual* concerns. No longer do I see a sea of faces confronting me. Their attitudes toward the class have become much more positive as have mine.

—sixth grade teacher

6.

I agree strongly with an open classroom atmosphere, and have used some of the suggested techniques previously. I added to their effectiveness with "I Learned . . . "Statements and grouping in different ways to get different students together, and observers.

Here are some lessons I have done with sixth graders:

1. Rank in order of importance to you: good student, good athletically, many friends, a few good friends, happy home life, very attractive, well-behaved, and wealthy. Discuss in groups with an observer to report on

each group interaction. Finally, write an "I Learn-ed . . ." statement.

2. Listen to a recording of *The Prince and the Pau-per* by Mark Twain. Write down something about your life you would like to change. Put all in a box. Then each person choose one and talk about it, pretending it is your own.

3. Write down in a list all your present and future ambitions. (I begin this with an article about a man who made a list of his ambitions when he was young and has completed many of them.) Check off which ones are possible, and which are probably not. Check the five you most want to achieve. Discuss and compare lists.

In the future I am anxious to try the continuum to increase speaking skills, and brainstorming ideas. I had already tried role-playing, but now with the open chair role-play, I think I can improve on it.

—sixth grade teacher

7.

The person on whom your *Composition for Person-al Growth* program has had the greatest impact is me. Certain activities have enabled me to learn a great deal about the kids at a deeper level, which I know is paying off with my being better able to bridge the communica-tion (and generation) gap. I believe I'm more effective in small-group and individualized work. I've had to re-think a great deal of my own values and attitudes and my teaching strategies and techniques—which has been a really good experience.

—English teacher, eighth grade